The Complete Magickal Bestiary

Long ago, strange and fabulous beasts filled the tales of storytellers and the myths of many cultures. Over time, humankind abandoned its connection with these powerful helpers.

This comprehensive guide describes the history, symbolism, appearance, associated traits, and magickal abilities of over two-hundred magickal creatures, and tells how to enlist their aid:

Unicorns • Centaurs • Satyrs and Fauns • Griffins • Goblins Magickal Serpents • Gigantic Birds • Gargoyles • Gremlins Fabulous Lions • The Ruhk • Mystical Bulls and Bull-Men Trolls • Pixies • Dwarfs • The Riddling Sphinx • Red Cap Hell Hounds • Water-Folk • Creatures of the Stony Stare The Salamander • Human-Birds • Fox Spirits • Flying Horses

Remember the forgotten magick—rediscover the unique abilities and powerful influence of the marvelous beings in *Magickal, Mystical Creatures.*

About the Author

I was born on a Beltane Full Moon with a total lunar eclipse, one of the hottest days of that year. Although I came into an Irish-North Germanic-Native American family with natural psychics on both sides, such abilities were not talked about. So I learned discrimination in a family of closet psychics.

I have always been close to Nature. Trees, herbs, and flowers are part of my indoor and outdoor landscapes wherever I live. I love cats, music, mountains, stones, ritual, reading, and nights when the Moon is full. I have studied every part of New Age religion from Eastern philosophy to Wicca. I hope I never stop learning and expanding.

I live a rather quiet life in the company of my husband and my six cats, with occasional visits with my children and grandchildren. Most of my time is spent researching and writing. Before I am finished with one book, I am working on another in my head. All in all, I am just an ordinary Pagan person.

To Write to the Author

If you wish to contact the author or would like more information about this book, please write to the author in care of Llewellyn Worldwide, and we will forward your request. Both the author and publisher appreciate hearing from you and learning of your enjoyment of this book. Llewellyn Worldwide cannot guarantee that every letter written to the author will be answered, but all will be forwarded. Please write to:

D. J. Conway
%Llewellyn Worldwide
P.O. Box 64383, Dept. K149–x, St. Paul, MN 55164-0383, U.S.A.
Please enclose a self-addressed stamped envelope for reply, or $1.00 to cover costs.
If outside U.S.A., enclose international postal reply coupon.

Magickal

Invite Their Powers

Mystical

into Your Life

Creatures

D. J. Conway

Llewellyn Publications
St. Paul, Minnesota

SECOND EDITION
Fifth printing, 2005

First edition, one printing, 1996.

Second edition cover design: William Merlin Cannon
Cover and interior art: Merle S. Insinga
Book design, layout, and editing: Jessica Thoreson

ISBN: 1-56718-149-x, Cataloging-in-Publication Data under previous title.
Library of Congress Cataloging-in-Publication Data
Magical, Mythical, mystical beasts: how to invite them into your life/D.J. Convway, —1st ed.
　　　p.　　cm
Includes bibliographical references and index.
ISBN: 1-56718-176-7 (pbk.)
　　　1. Magic. 2. Animals, Mythical—Miscellanea. 3. Ritual. I. Title
BF1623.A55C67 1996
398'.469—DC20　　　　　　　　　　　　　　　　　　　96-9051
　　　　　　　　　　　　　　　　　　　　　　　　　　　　CIP

Llewellyn Publications
A Division of Llewellyn Worldwide, Ltd.
P.O. Box 64383
Dept. 1-56718-149-x
St. Paul, MN 55164-0383
http://www.llewellyn.com

Printed in the United States of America

Other Books by the Author

Celtic Magic
Norse Magic
Magick of the Gods & Goddesses
        (formerly *The Ancient & Shining Ones*)
Maiden, Mother, Crone
Dancing With Dragons
By Oak, Ash, & Thorn
Animal Magick
Flying Without a Broom
Moon Magick
Falcon Feather & Valkyrie Sword
Astral Love
The Dream Warrior (fiction)
Lord of Light & Shadow
Soothslayer (fiction)
The Mysterious, Magickal Cat
Shapeshifter Tarot (with Sirona Knight)
Celtic Dragon Tarot (with Lisa Hunt)

Table of Contents

Part 1

The Forgotten Magick

Introduction

Nearly everyone has heard of certain magickal, mythical creatures of the world, Unicorns and Dragons being the most popular. However, there are a great many more such beasts and creatures whose existence is little known or has been forgotten. This was brought to my attention when my book *Dancing With Dragons* was released in the fall of 1994. I was not prepared for the enthusiasm with which the book was received by the reading public. Several letters asked the same questions: When are you going to write about Unicorns (or some other fabulous beast)? What about all the other magickal creatures?

There are already so many books about Unicorns that I simply could not see doing an entire book on that subject. I am well acquainted with Pegasus, the Minotaur, the Sphinx, and several other beings through my mythological studies, but I began to wonder if there were others I had forgotten or never heard about.

It seems when I wrote *Dancing With Dragons* and *Animal Magick*, the doors to the hidden world of other creatures opened wide. Suddenly, everywhere I turned, some strange mythical creature demanded my attention. I seldom opened a book without some reference catching my eye. Nearly every catalog I read or store I visited seemed to have at least one mythical creature. The rapport I had established previously with Dragons and animal familiars was an introduction to a whole world of critters I had not thought much about before.

I mentioned all this to Nancy Mostad at Llewellyn, and she replied, "Why not write a book about them?" So I began collecting notes and ideas and started an outline, not in any great hurry about this possible future book project. Then at Winter Solstice a gift arrived from a long-time friend. Inside was a Gargoyle, and he was very much alive in the psychic sense. I immediately gave him the job of watching the entire property and the front door in particular.

What could I do? It was obvious these fabulous creatures had something to say. My magickal curiosity was stirred up. I decided to write a "Who's Who" of magickal, mythical, mystical beasts, an introduction and history of these fabulous creatures and how they, like the Dragons, can be co-magicians in magickal workings. The only similar books I have found are the old bestiaries, which are all highly Christianized and have nothing to do with magick. As far as I know, this is a "one-of-a-kind" book on the subject.

Not everyone who reads this book, or hears about it, will understand and believe as I do about the Otherworlds of magickal creatures and beings. Nor will they relate to such creatures in the same way. Everyone must seek the path of understanding that is right for them. However, I do hope you will keep an open, non-critical mind, accepting what you feel is right for you and allowing others to accept what is right for them without comment.

Welcome to the world of fabulous, magickal creatures who are still alive and well and very powerful in the astral planes.

1

What Are the Magickal, Mystical Creatures?

In records and carvings from thousands of years ago we find the first mention of strange, fabulous beasts. It is evident that early cultures knew these creatures well, although most of the surviving written records are sketchy. In some instances, there are only statues or carvings and few words about several creatures.

Many magickal beasts are mentioned in mythology and folklore, some in greater detail than others. Nearly everyone is familiar with the Unicorn and Dragon, the Sphinx and the Phoenix. But how many people are aware of the Shedu of ancient Mesopotamia, the Cu Sith of Scotland, the Barbegazi of Switzerland, or the

Firebird of Russia? There are many fascinating mythical creatures waiting to be rediscovered.

There always arise the strongly debated questions: were these fabulous beasts ever "real" animals in the physical world? If they were "real," do they still exist? If they exist, why can't we see them now or catch one of them?

Some of the creatures in this book have been sighted up through the present day. The people who see the creatures are not drunk, drugged, mentally unbalanced, or anything other than ordinary people who mostly don't believe in such things.

Like Dragons, these beings may have, at one time, been more at ease in our world, regularly interacting with humans. Then, when they found humans becoming more aggressive, violent, and untrustworthy, they withdrew to the astral plane from which they came. Now, their appearances in the physical world to human eyes are rare, but they can appear, if they so desire.

Some people will say that these creatures are imaginary, nothing more. Even if this is so, which it isn't, magicians know that strong, deliberate creations of the imagination can take on form and personality if the visualization is repeated over a long period of time on a regular basis, or if the magician is strong enough. I challenge anyone who has called upon a Dragon or one of the Shedu to say it isn't real after you have felt it breathe down the back of your neck.

As with Dragons, these mythical, mystical beings at one time had greater contact with humans than they do now. Ancient cultures believed it was possible to make direct contact with astral beings and creatures, something now looked upon as foolishness by a great many of the unenlightened. Because of unbelief and skepticism (which usually translate into hostility), astral creatures have found it advantageous to keep within their own realm and avoid most humans. After all, if an astral being manifests itself clearly enough to be seen or at least felt, the usual reaction by close-minded humans is to attack. The aggressiveness and unpredictability of the average human is enough to cause most astral creatures to remain hidden from sight and avoid contact.

Acknowledgement of the creature's existence and power appears to have a direct bearing upon whether or not a magician (or any person) ever meets or feels the presence of such a creature. Also important is the reaction of such a person when the creature appears. If you call upon the Shedu, for example, and suddenly feel their enormous presence towering over you, great wings creating a draft and huge hooves tapping on your floor, the last thing you want to do is run screaming from your ritual circle. If you read the section on the Shedu, you would realize this is insulting behavior on your part. You will never make their acquaintance or get them to help you.

It is rare for any astral creature or being to appear in a manner that can be seen with the physical eyes. Astral beings are of a totally different vibration than matter on this Earth plane of existence. However, on occasion, they may make a partial appearance (becoming visible within your mind), but are more likely to signal their presence by feelings or sounds. Just because you are unable to see such creatures with your physical eyes does not mean they do not exist. You cannot see bacteria or viruses (good or bad), either. Atoms cannot be seen at all, even with the most powerful microscopes. But they all exist in their own realms and ways, and they all affect us.

In ancient times, before the "modern" religions drove out this knowledge, humans called upon these wonderful magickal creatures for aid. Enlightened humans and magicians knew the esoteric meanings behind each of these creatures. They knew that working with or calling upon specific creatures from the astral would also have psychological benefits. How sad it is to know that we have been deliberately deprived of these mystical beasts and their great knowledge.

The strange beasts of mythology and folklore, the human-beasts, and the otherworldly little creatures who fit into no category but their own are waiting for humans to reaffirm and acknowledge their existence. They cannot only be co-magicians and helpers, but teachers and healers at a time when humans need all the help they can get. Their growth and ours appear to be intertwined in some way; we need each other.

Merely recognizing them after centuries of neglect is pleasing to them. But they are still waiting for magicians to learn how to work with them once again. Magick and teaching seem to be of great interest and importance to these magickal, mythical beings. Whether you are reading for pleasure or for a way to increase your magickal knowledge, I hope you find this book a fascinating adventure.

2

Working With the Magickal Beasts

Reading about these magickal, mythical creatures is an engrossing pastime. It can be a
personal adventure, a return to childhood
freedom of thought, to read about these unfamiliar
beings, and even more exciting when one discovers
a previously unknown beast. In a way it is a temporary escape from the sometimes harsh realities in
which we live. Simply reading about these fabulous
creatures, and daydreaming about them and the
times when they had influence, allows us to release
stress and regroup our hopes and dreams of a better
future. However, escapism is not the only reason we
are fascinated by these mythical, mystical beings.

Humankind remains interested in Unicorns,
Dragons, the Sphinx, and the Minotaur—all well
known from classical and medieval mythologies—
because of the superconscious mind which is part of

each of us. The superconscious mind (the repository of all racial memories to which we all have access) remembers ancient times when our world and the world of these mystical creatures were in greater communication than they are today. So we are fascinated and hold subconscious thoughts of re-establishing that communication.

Not everyone who reads this book will wish to call upon these magickal creatures and work with them. Some people will read merely for entertainment, not because it is part of the current fad to do so. You can read this book in this manner, for fun, and not be concerned about working magick.

However, a knowledgeable magician can use this book to learn how to contact and befriend these mythical beasts, enlisting their aid in magickal spellworkings and rituals. Where caution is needed with certain creatures, appropriate warnings are given. I recommend that you call upon most of the magickal beasts within a cast circle, especially if you desire a semi-manifestation of their presence. Casting such a circle not only signifies your serious magickal intent, but also helps protect you should you lose your concentration while working with some of the more difficult creatures.

Ritual is not the only way to work with these creatures. If you want to use just the power and influence of the more benign creatures, you can create an amulet or talisman. This "charm" can be hung in your home, your car, or on your body. If you would like a particular creature to work with you in fulfilling a desire, do a candle burning. All these methods are described in Part III.

Every magician should develop self-discipline, patience, and responsibility before becoming involved in any type of magick, particularly when working with any of the magickal beasts. As when working with Dragons, the magician does not try for a master-slave relationship, but one of partnership. I stressed this about Dragon magick,[1] and I emphasize this again. If you try to dominate a magickal creature instead of developing an attitude of mutual cooperation, you will be in for some unpleasant surprises.

Several things could happen if you try domination. The magickal beasts could ignore you and not help at all. Your spellworkings could misfire, and you could get a result you did not want. Or things could really backfire, and you could find yourself plagued by all kinds of negative experiences.

Some of these fabulous creatures are trickier than others to work with, and should be approached with great care. A few are so mischievous that you must be totally clear in your mind and words exactly what you plan to accomplish. Otherwise, they will take advantage of your hesitancies and ambiguities to create a result they want—usually one of minor chaos in your life just to watch you struggle through it.

So why would you want to work with these mythical creatures at all? Because they, as powerful astral beings, have access to energy which can augment a magician's spells in a new way. Often the Otherworld energies and powers these creatures bring are the only things that will break through barriers preventing you from moving ahead in your magickal pursuits or in life itself. They can work changes in your environment and your life. This includes not only the physical realm, but the mental and spiritual realms as well.

Each chapter has sections on both the psychological and magickal attributes of these mythical creatures. The psychological uses are somewhat complex. This section often has both a negative and positive definition for each creature. The word "negative" is used to describe the less desirable traits associated with the creature or creatures. By being brutally honest with yourself, which every magician must be, when you read the negative psychological section you can determine if you are harboring undesirable personality traits associated with the Sphinx, for example. The Sphinx had a nasty reputation for toying with its victims before killing them. You can offset such a trait by deliberately focusing on a positive characteristic, such as the wisdom of the Sphinx and its being the guardian of the gateway to initiation.

Reading through the characteristics of these mythical creatures may also help you better understand the traits exhibited by people who trouble you. Once you see through their psychological games, you can keep from being a victim.

The magickal uses are fairly self-explanatory: a magician calls upon a particular creature and asks for help in creating a certain result.

Each magickal beast listed in this book has a slightly different realm of expertise. It is best to read all about a particular creature before trying to work with it. Think of this book as a guidebook to a strange land of very different inhabitants. You want to keep on the good side of these inhabitants and not offend them unknowingly, thereby incurring their displeasure.

Ancient magicians once worked with the magickal, mythical, mystical beasts and creatures. As with so much ancient occult knowledge, information about those beings was lost, forgotten, or deliberately destroyed over the centuries. In this era, when magick and Paganism are again practiced with sincerity, it is important that this knowledge be made available to those who are willing to practice self-discipline, patience, and responsibility. A magician must be willing to take care of his or her own problems or challenges in life, and this ancient knowledge will enable you to do just that.

For those who are not interested in magick, read for enjoyment. For those who intend to work magick, read to regain the hidden ancient knowledge. Either way, be prepared to meet some fascinating astral beings who are still alive in their own realm and full of power.

ENDNOTES

1. Conway, D. J. *Dancing With Dragons.*

Part II

Fabulous Beasts

3

Unicorns

The Unicorn, along with the Dragon, is perhaps the most popular and well-known of the fabulous beasts, especially in the Western Hemisphere. This is primarily because the medieval Christians adopted the Unicorn and changed its symbolic meanings to fit into their religion. To them, it became a symbol of their Christ, something the Unicorn never was originally. They made the Dragon symbolize their devil.

Fascination with the Unicorn continues right down to today. For example, the animated movie *The Last Unicorn,* based on a book by Peter Beagle,[1] is still popular. Statues and pictures of Unicorns are readily available in gift shops. There are a great many books about Unicorns. The Unicorn, along with other fabulous beasts, can also be found in several role-playing games.

The Unicorn is one of the few fabulous mythical beasts with a shape considered realistic by our human terms. In other words, we are able to visualize the Unicorn as a creature we could possibly meet. Some people want to see and own a Unicorn so badly that they have resorted to an ancient minor surgical method by which they, quite literally, transform two-horned goats and cattle into one-horned creatures. These Unicorns are not true Unicorns.

Some of the ancient horse-tribes of central Asia believed so strongly in the Unicorn and its magickal influence and strength that they outfitted their mounts with leather headpieces bearing an artificial horn. Horse skulls wearing these have been discovered in Siberian burial sites.[2] Some early European horse-armor also has a horn on the forehead plate of the headpiece.

To discover the description of a true Unicorn we must search far back in ancient history, writings, and mythology. When we do this, we find that the description and size of Unicorns differ according to the culture and land where it made its appearance, just as there are differences in other animals from continent to continent.

Many historians claim that the ancients did not know the difference between the gazelle-like Unicorn and the rhinoceros or the antelopes seen in ancient paintings. They totally ignore the fact that the ancient peoples had separate names for the antelope, rhinoceros, and Unicorn.

The word Unicorn literally means "one-horned," and comes from two Latin words, *unus,* "one;" and *cornu,* "horn." Thus, the Unicorn is a unique creature with only one natural horn in the center of its forehead. The Unicorn is not an animal that has broken off one horn or the rhinoceros, which has a horn on the end of its long face. It is not a creature that has been surgically altered so both its natural horns grow together in the center of its forehead. A Unicorn is a creature of a specific species which has only one natural horn, a creature which has never been tamed, owned, or bred by humans.

This creature has been depicted and seen in such places as China, Mongolia, the Middle East, Egypt, North Africa, India, Japan, Europe, Florida, along the Canadian border, and in many other places around the world. Their distribution appeared to be limited to the Northern Hemisphere.

Pliny wrote that the Unicorn lived in India, while Herodotus said it existed in Libya. Ethiopians claimed to have seen Unicorns living in the Upper Nile regions. The Tibetans wrote of Unicorns in their area, and the Arabs knew this animal well.

In Greek and Roman art, the goddess Artemis/Diana was often shown in a chariot pulled by eight Unicorns. This connection with the Moon goddesses was seen in art as far back as the time of the Sumero-Semitic civilizations.

The European version of this animal was said to have the head and body of a horse, the hind legs of an antelope or stag, the whiskers of a goat, the tail of a lion, and a long, spiral horn in the middle of its forehead. A few writers said that the horn was straight instead of spiralled. Vertomannus, Albertus Magnus, and Strabo all wrote that it had split hooves like those of a goat, while some medieval illustrations show it with cloven hooves on its front legs, but solid hooves on its back legs. Medieval writers gave detailed descriptions of the Unicorn, which later found their way into the depiction of the Unicorn in heraldry.

Many writers differed on the color of European Unicorns. Most said it was a pure white, while others, accepting one of the descriptions from India, said it had a white body, red head, and blue eyes.

UNICORN

The European Unicorn lived in the temperate forests of Europe and was so swift that no hunter could catch it. It generally lived alone, the males and females coming together only for mating. The colt, born without a horn, stayed with its mother until its horn was full length. Although usually a gentle creature, a Unicorn would use its sharp horn to defend its territory.

European writers disagreed on the color of the horn. Before the sixteenth century, they declared that the true horn was all black. Later it was said to be white or the color of old ivory. Thomas Fuller put forth the idea that the differences in color could be accounted for by age: white on the younger Unicorns, ivory when they were at least one hundred years old, and black when older. Other naturalists of the time wrote that the true horn was white inside with a black, bark-like exterior.

Although a few writers mentioned straight Unicorn horns, the majority called them spiralled, twisted, or striated. Even the Unicorns shown in the bas-reliefs of ancient Persepolis have twisted horns. The Arabian writer Alkazuwin confirmed this.

Critics often argue that the ancient depictions of Unicorns are of a two-horned animal seen from the side with one horn revealed. However, Robert Brown discovered that the ancient peoples depicted two-horned animals looking to the right, while the one-horned Unicorn was always shown looking to the left. In heraldry, this posture is known as regardant.

In European stories, there are many accounts of Unicorns being hunted for their horns, which were considered to detect and be an antidote for poisons. The horn (sometimes called an Alicorn) also purified water; dipped into a pool of muddy water, the water would become clear. Any person who drank from a Unicorn horn would have good health all his life, besides avoiding being poisoned. Because of these qualities, ancient rulers paid great sums for Unicorn horns. Unicorn's horn became an essential item in apothecaries until the eighteenth century. Powdered horns were worth ten times their weight in gold, while the whole horn was nearly beyond price.

Two Unicorn horns are still in St. Mark's church in Venice, now very thin from repeated scrapings. Another is kept in a dark vault in the French Cathedral of St. Denis; it is said to be so potent that water in which the horn is steeped can cure any illness. A Unicorn horn was listed in the inventory of the treasure of Charles I. Another such horn was once kept at Windsor Castle, where it could be viewed by travelers to the court of Elizabeth I; its value at that time was 100,000 pounds.

Since Unicorn horns sold for vast amounts of money, fakes were often on the market. One method used to distinguish the true from the false was to inscribe a circle on the ground around a horn and then put a scorpion, spider, or lizard inside the circle. A true Unicorn horn would prevent the creature from escaping.

The *Physiologus Graecus* says this creature harbored ill-will toward humans, and with good cause. Although Western people believed that the Unicorn was a lunar creature, gentle and wise, they still hunted it with great determination. They soon found that snares, spears, and bows were useless for hunting Unicorns. In order to trap it, a beautiful young virgin was set as bait; the Unicorn was said to come to her willingly. While she held its head in her lap, the hunters would either kill the animal or saw off its horn.

Ctesias, a Greek physician, went to the court of the Persian king Darius II in 416 B.C.E.[3] and stayed for seventeen years as a court physician. When he returned to Greece, he recorded both the local stories and the Unicorn tales told to him by visitors from India. These travelers described the Indian Unicorn as having a white horse-body, a dark red head, and dark blue eyes. He estimated the horn on its forehead to be about one-and-a-half feet long. This horn was tri-colored: pure white on the bottom for some two hands' spans, black in the middle, and a vivid red at the sharp tip. The ankle bone was said to be very heavy, like lead, and a cinnabar color completely through the bone.

Since Ctesias had spent seventeen years in Persia, he was well acquainted with the wild ass which ran wild in that region. Regardless of later detractors' opinions, he knew the difference between this creature and a Unicorn. The traveler reported that dust filed from the horn and made into a potion was an antidote to deadly drugs, while drinking from the horn gave immunity to epilepsy and poisons.

The naturalist Aelian, in the third century C.E., journeyed to India and saw the creatures described by Ctesias. However, he described the Unicorn as having reddish-yellow hair and a black horn with a natural twist to it. He wrote that the Brahmins there called the Unicorn the Cartazonon, and that it was a solitary animal found in desert regions. While there, he also heard first-hand about the medicinal properties of Unicorn horn. The Indians made cups out of the horn as protection against several sicknesses and poison. He described the horn as having rings around it.

The elder Pliny also mentioned the Indian Unicorn, which he called the monoceros. He said the Indians hunted this swift, powerful creature primarily for its horn. Pliny's description is similiar to that given by Ctesias, except Ctesias said the horn was all black. Later writers tried to say that this monoceros was only a rhinoceros, but it is difficult to believe one could possibly mistake one for the other.

The Greek Aristotle wrote that he knew of several different types of Unicorns. He classified these into two categories: those with cloven hooves, like the oryx, and those with solid hooves, like the Indian ass.

An early report of European Unicorns came from Julius Caesar while he was campaigning in the Hercynian Forest of Germany. In his Gallic Wars he describes the creature as shaped like a stag, the size of an ox, with a single horn between its ears.

In 1389, John of Hesse visited Palestine, where he saw a Unicorn dip its horn into a river to purify the water. Nearly a century later, Felix Fabri saw another Unicorn near Mount Sinai. In 1502, a man named Lewis Vartoman came upon several Unicorns in a park in Mecca. Vertomannus, who traveled to Mecca in 1503, wrote of Unicorns in the Temple there.

In the sixth century C.E., at the court of the King of Ethiopia, Cosmas Indicopleustes saw four bronze statues of the Unicorn and was told that this creature existed. A seventeenth-century Portuguese missionary, Jieronymo Lobo, saw several Unicorns in Ethiopia.

Recent excavations at Ur of the Chaldees revealed a beautiful lady's toilet-box. The lid of this box was done in gold and lapis lazuli, showing a lion locked in combat with a one-horned beast.

The British Museum has a magnificent bas-relief from Assyria showing the king Assurbanipal hunting Unicorns.

A surviving record written by an unknown Chinese traveler of the eleventh or twelfth century tells of seeing a great many Unicorns near a lake in Tibet. As late as 1820, a Major Latta, who was in the British Army, wrote home that he had seen a Unicorn in Tibet and that these creatures were known as the Tso'Po.

Genghis Kahn, in 1224, personally met a Unicorn at the top of Mount Djadanaring in Hindustan. He considered its appearance so important that he terminated his campaign for conquest of the region.

Aldrovandus reported seeing a Unicorn in Poland, while Johnston, in the *Historia Naturalis,* wrote of the Unicorns of Scandinavia.

However, Unicorn sightings are not confined to the Middle East or Europe. The conquistadors, while exploring Florida, saw Unicorns. Two men (one of them Sir John Hawkins) reported seeing a Unicorn in Florida in the sixteenth century. A hundred years later, Dr. Olfert Dapper wrote of several Unicorn sightings in Maine and along the Canadian border. These sightings always occurred in rural areas. Dr. Dapper described the creatures as resembling horses, but with cloven hooves, rough manes, a single horn on the forehead, and black eyes.

There are several recorded gifts of one-horned creatures given to people, usually as a sign of the recipient's power. A one-horned ram was given to the Greek Pericles as a sign of his leadership. An Ethiopian king sent two Unicorns to the Sultan of Mecca in the fifteenth century, and the Elector of Saxony was given the gift of a Unicorn in the seventeenth century.

The European people of the Middle Ages believed that, besides the curative and protective powers of the horn, the Unicorn had another special feature. At the base of the horn, they said, was a magickal carbuncle, which they called a ruby. This carbuncle was thought to have powerful properties useful in both magick and healing, including protection from the plague.

Unicorns have been pictured in great detail in European art. The Unicorn was a part of the arms of the Apothecaries Society as well as of the Goldsmiths. The British royal coat of arms in 1693 showed a traditional Unicorn, as did the Lady and the Unicorn tapestry of about 1480 in France.

The Unicorn is depicted in woodcuts, heraldry, and illuminated manuscripts, both on the Continent and in Britain. In heraldry, the Unicorn is the most beautiful of all the fabulous creatures used. In this type of art it is depicted with the body, head, and mane of a horse, a goat's beard on its chin, the legs and cloven hooves[4] of a deer, the tail of a lion, and a long, spiral single horn on its forehead. Normally it is colored white, with a golden horn, hooves, mane, and tail-tuft.

The symbolism of the Unicorn depends on the culture and the religion defining it. To the Christians, the creature meant virginity, purity, and innocence; these definitions were related to their God and Jesus. In the Orient, however, the Unicorn was a symbol of good will, benevolence, longevity, and wise administration.

Unicorns might shun humans, except those of pure heart, but the creatures do have contact with the Elves, Faeries, and elemental woodland spirits, such as Dryads. Often they will consent to being temporary steeds for dimensional journeys. They move so silently that they often surprise those seeking them.

As an untamed creature with strong elemental powers, the Unicorn, in general, is a symbol of transformation. It purifies through the powers of destruction. As with the Crone aspect of the Goddess, the Unicorn "destroys" in order to re-create. It tears down in order to reform and renew. We may find the process unsettling, harsh, and even painful, but it is necessary to get rid of old cycles and prepare for new ones.

Unicorns guard the way to the Faery realms and can guide you there if you are prepared for the experience.

Psychological Attributes: Positive—Proper working with Unicorns should have a tremendous impact on your morality, sense of propriety, and spiritual growth. Unicorns will not help those who are not interested in cleaning up their personal morals. If your life has been average (good and bad by turns), the appearance of a Unicorn will signal a coming change of great importance. This change may be positive or negative, but it will have a profound impact on the way you live your life. Negative—Over-defensive all the time; verbally or physically attacking anyone you imagine is a possible threat.

Magickal Attributes: Good will, fame, prosperity, gentleness, purity, strength of mind. Unlimited individual power. For wisdom combined with success. Developing personal power.

Ch'i-lin

The Chinese Unicorn was called Ch'i-lin, Ky-lin, or K'i-lin, and was very different in appearance from the European Unicorn. This Oriental creature had the head of a Dragon, the tail of an ox, and a stag's body. Its skin was red, yellow, blue, white, and black. These colors symbolized the Ch'i-lin's magickal connection with the five elements: fire, water, wood, metal, and earth. They said this creature was no larger than a goat but was fierce and had great strength. When it made a noise, it sounded like bells.

Chinese legend says this Unicorn lived for a thousand years and came to China from a far place. The Chinese considered it to be the noblest of animals and did not hunt it, as did the Western cultures. As a later emblem of high birth and good character, it became a symbol of high-ranking army officers.

There are many surviving pictures or statues of Chinese Unicorns. While the written description of the Ch'i-lin is fairly consistent, artistic portrayals vary. One Chinese ink on paper picture is of a type of one-horned Ch'i-lin with a lion-like body and legs, no hooves, a single horn, and an upward-standing, feathery, flame-like mane around its head. Sometimes it was shown with two horns. One of these drawings, from the late Ch'ing

CH'I-LIN

Dynasty in China, shows a creature with two branched horns, an elaborate beard, hooves, and featherlike scales covering its body and legs. A cloisonne figure depicts the Ch'i-lin with two branched horns, a curled beard, a thin tail with a fluffy end, and a small, antelope-like body.

In both China and Japan, the male was called the *k'i*, or *ch'i*, the female the *lin*, or *rin*. To correctly speak of the species, one would say the Ch'i-lin. It was known as the most perfect of all the land animals.

Ancient Chinese mythology tells that P'an Ku, the first man, took centuries to create the order of the universe out of the original state of chaos. Four special animals—the Dragon, tortoise, Phoenix, and the Ch'i-lin—helped him in his task. These were considered fortunate animals. When P'an Ku died, his body became the world and these creatures were free to seek their own places. The Dragon went into the seas, the tortoise the swamps, and the Phoenix the dry land. The Ch'i-lin ran into the green forests where it only revealed itself to humans on special occasions. Although the territories of these animals are described in human terms, the Chinese say that they inhabit hidden realms where their special powers will not be diminished by contact with humans.

There are only two reasons for the Ch'i-lin to reveal itself. As a prophetic creature, it will appear in the forest to an observer when times are peaceful and prosperous under the rule of a good leader. It will also appear when a great leader is about to die.

The emperor Fu Hsi saw a Ch'i-lin around 280 B.C.E as he sat beside the Yellow River. He wrote that the Ch'i-lin looked like a calf but had gleaming scales like a Dragon. On its forehead was a silvery horn. On its back were magickal signs; Fu Hsi carefully copied them down. With these signs and his knowledge of the movement of the stars, he created the first written Chinese language.[5] As the Ch'i-lin walked through the muddy water, the river became like clear green glass. The creature came to stand in front of the emperor, stamped its hoof three times on a rock, and cried out in a voice like a monastery bell.

The Ch'i-lin was also seen by a later emperor, Huang Ti, as his death neared. A few of his successors also caught a glimpse of this creature.

A young woman named Ching-tsae saw this creature 2000 years later while she worshipped in an ancient temple. The Ch'i-lin gave her a piece of green jade and prophesied that she would bear a son who would become a great but throneless king. She later became the mother of Kung Fu Sze, or Confucius. It was also said that the Unicorn reappeared when Confucius died.

Wu Ti, an emperor of the Han Dynasty, 400 years after Confucius, caught a brief glimpse of a pure white Ch'i-lin on his palace grounds. He was so excited by this short encounter that he built a special pagoda to honor the creature and in hopes that it would return. However, he never saw it again.

The Chinese say that the Ch'i-lin no longer appears because there is no virtue in China's leaders anymore. However, they still use the saying, "May the Unicorn's hoof bring you good luck."

Psychological Attributes: Positive—Dignity; good character; fierceness in defense of good; great spiritual strength. Only appears on special occasions. Negative—One who likes to predict doom and gloom about the plans or hopes of others.

Magickal Attributes: Good fortune, connection with the five Elements, prophecy.

Ki-rin

One form of the Japanese Unicorn was called the Ki-rin and is similar to the creature described by the Chinese. This solitary creature was said to walk with a dignified step or, on rare occasions, skip along when it moved.

One Japanese depiction of the Ki-rin, on an ivory plectrum of the eighth century, shows a creature with a horse-like body, a single horn, and flame-like wings on its front shoulders and flanks. The coat of the Ki-rin is composed of delicate feathers or feather-like scales, which are either a luminous golden brown or simply gold. Its mane and tail are of a darker gold, as are its horn and hooves. The eyes are a beautiful blue-violet or warm sunny brown.

The Oriental type of Unicorn is also represented in Buddhist temple paintings and sculptures.

Psychological Attributes: See Ch'i-lin.

Magickal Attributes: See Ch'i-lin.

Sin-you

Another Japanese Unicorn is known as the Sin-you. The fierce Sin-you looks like a lion with a thick, tawny mane and a single horn. It also has the ability to know who is guilty and who is innocent. The sage Kau You consulted the Sin-you regarding the serious law cases which came before him in his court. This creature would stand still and stare with its sun-flecked eyes at the guilty party. Then suddenly it would pierce the guilty person through the heart with its horn.

Psychological Attributes: Positive—Establishing innocence; working within moral and spiritual laws. Negative—Too quick in judgment.

Magickal Attributes: Learning to detect when someone is lying; bringing the guilty to justice.

Karkadann

In Arabia and ancient Persia lived another type of Unicorn called the Karkadann. Sometimes it was described as resembling a stag,

KARKADANN

horse, or antelope. Other times it was said to have a body like a rhinoceros, a tail like a lion, and yellow hooves, with a single, black, crescent-shaped horn on its forehead. Legend says it was born by tearing its way through its mother's body. Therefore, the Arabs and Persians said the Karkadann was a war-like, violent animal, ferocious in battle beyond compare. Because of its aggressive temperament and its loud, harsh voice, all living creatures left it alone. Even so, its flesh, fat, and horn were thought to have miraculous healing and protective powers.

The people living in what was once known as Abyssinia knew of the Unicorn. Fray Luis de Urreta wrote that Unicorns lived in what was known as the Mountains of the Moon in that region. The Arabs who later lived in that region also had a strong belief in these creatures and told stories about them.

The ancient Macedonians believed that Alexander the Great's mount, Bucephalus, was a Unicorn. The nobles who captured the animal and took it to Alexander's father, Philip, called it a Karkadann. However, this animal was said to have the body of a horse and a single straight horn on its head, unlike the Karkadann, which had a crescent-shaped horn. After his father and several other men failed to ride the creature, Alexander talked gently to it, then mounted it and rode off. Bucephalus remained his treasured mount through all his Far Eastern campaigns.

Psychological Attributes: Positive—Having the inner strength to defend yourself. Negative—A person who has a violent nature; one who loves to cause upset, turmoil, even creating violence and hatred between other people.

Magickal Attributes: Healing; protection.

Goat-Unicorns

Two kinds of Unicorns were known in Egypt. Physiologus, who lived in Egypt some time between the second and fifth centuries C.E., wrote a bestiary in which he described Unicorns. Besides the usual Unicorn, he described another kind which was the size of a goat with a beard and cloven hooves. However, Brunetto Latini, an ency-clopedist, made a detailed distinction between horse-like Unicorns and a gigantic one-horned goat which he called an Elisserion.

One of the most famous present-day surgically altered Goat-Unicorns was raised by Otter and Morning Glory Gazelle. It is the size of an ordinary goat and is quite beautiful.

Psychological Attributes: Positive—See Unicorn. Negative—Using Unicorn qualities to satisfy your physical lusts.

Magickal Attributes: Determination; gentleness.

Winged Sea-Unicorn

The winged Sea-Unicorn of heraldry is a strange composite creature about whom little is known. It is shown with the front part, head, and forelegs of a horse, a fish-tail in the rear, and a Unicorn's horn on its head. However, it also has wings on its front shoulders.

Working with the winged Sea-Unicorn can help you prepare your emotions for deep magickal work.

Psychological Attributes: Positive—One who can combine the positive qualities of the Unicorn and Pegasus for control over his or her emotions. Negative—A person who manipulates the emotions of others.

Magickal Attributes: Getting control over an emotional situation which, left unchecked, may lead to more upheaval and negative feelings.

ENDNOTES

1. *The Last Unicorn.* NY: Viking, 1968.
2. Davidson, H. R. Ellis. *Pagan Scandinavia.*
3. B.C.E. means Before Common Era; C.E. means Common Era. This is a non-religious method of dating replacing the Christianized B.C. and A.D.
4. Brown, Robert. *Semitic Influence in Hellenic Mythology.*
5. Some versions say Fu Hsi got the signs from the back of a tortoise.

4

Flying Horses

Winged horses have long been part of mythology in many cultures. They are usually directly connected with deities in one way or another, often acting as celestial messengers. When speaking of winged horses, Pegasus immediately comes to mind. However, there were other flying horses about which little is known by the average person.

Any winged horse is symbolic of humankind's inborn ability to travel from one realm of being to another in the astral body to discover ancient spiritual knowledge. Mythical winged horses can also help you escape any dangers you might encounter within the astral realms.

Pegasus

The winged horse Pegasus, from the Greek myths, is a familiar magickal, mythical creature. He was a white horse with golden (sometimes white) wings and the ability to fly.

Several myths give different versions of the origin of this mag-
ickal horse. One legend says Pegasus was born from the blood of
Medusa after Perseus cut off her head. Another version states that
Pegasus sprang from the blood-soaked earth after the death of
Medusa, while yet another says that Poseidon created the horse by
mixing Medusa's blood with sand. A much older story tells that
Pegasus sprang from the menstrual blood of the Gorgon Medusa.

Another story says Medusa was pregnant with two children by
Poseidon when Perseus killed her. At her death, her children sprang
full-grown from her body. One child was Pegasus; the other was a
human warrior named Chrysaor. Pegasus immediately escaped to
Mount Helicon where the Muses took him in. Nothing is said about
what Chrysaor did.

If Pegasus and the magickal horse Arion (Moon creature on
high) were the same being, then Pegasus was born of the Greek goddess Demeter when she was raped by Poseidon. Very early records tell
of a female Pegasus named Aganippe, which is often given as the
name for Demeter in her destroying aspect of the Night-mare.

The idea of Pegasus may have originated in Egypt, where the
ancient shrine of Osiris at Abydos (about 2000 B.C.E.) held a sacred
spring called Pega.[1] This Osiris cult may have branched off later to
Corinth, where the sacred spring of Pirene (Hippocrene) was
tended by the water-priestesses known as the Pegae. These priestesses wore horse-masks. A Greek legend states that the Fountain of
Hippocrene (the Moon-Horse well or spring) on Mount Helicon,
which belonged to the Muses, was created when Pegasus struck the
ground there with his hoof. It was believed that anyone who rode
Pegasus could become a great poet.

Pegasus was graceful, beautiful, wise, and gentle. He was so
pure he could reach directly to the gates of Olympus, yet he sometimes assisted human heroes, such as Perseus and Bellerophon. This
magickal flying horse helped Bellerophon conquer and slay the
Chimera.[2] This victory, however, went to Bellerophon's head and he
tried to ride Pegasus into the realm of the gods. Zeus sent a gadfly to
sting Pegasus, who threw his rider to his death. Finally, Pegasus took

PEGASUS

his place among the constellations of stars. It is possible that Pegasus produced offspring before he went into the heavens.

In pre-Christian times, Pegasus was the emblem of the Greek city-state of Corinth. During the Renaissance, this creature began to be used on European armor, then found its way into heraldry.

Pegasus, more than any other flying horse, symbolizes the human need to rise above the mundane physical in which we live most of our lives, and the subconscious desire to seek spiritual answers and set spiritual goals.

Psychological Attributes: Positive—One with the natural ability to change evil into good. Negative—A person who feels superior to others because of his or her knowledge.

Magickal Attributes: Poetic inspiration; learning astral travel. Changing evil into good. Riding Pegasus in meditation or astral travel to the Otherworlds can help bring poetic inspiration. Fame, eloquence. Taking a soul journey to the Moon or Underworld to learn great secrets of life and magick. Visiting with deceased souls.

Winged Sea-Pegasus

The winged Sea-Pegasus has horse's hooves on its forelegs, but the back parts of a fish. The seahorse in its many mythical forms (not the tiny seahorse we know) was often called up by Poseidon/Neptune when this sea god struck the ocean with his trident, creating storms and high, foam-capped waves.

Although the seahorse is primarily seen in ancient Greek and Roman art, it was also known to the Celts. In Celtic mythology, the sea-chariot of Manannan mac Lir was pulled by these magickal creatures. Seahorses are also associated with the Water-Folk of the seas.

The winged Sea-Pegasus represents the inborn need of humans to seek spiritual solutions to intense emotional problems. Pegasus may represent the desire to transcend the physical and intellect in the search for spiritual growth, but Sea-Pegasus symbolizes our desire to transcend the controlling, but subtle, grasp of emotions which keep us locked into a series of lives and problems.

Winged sea-horses can help you to escape dangerous and/or limiting emotional entanglements.

Psychological Attributes: Positive—A person who uses spiritual techniques to change and/or rise above personal emotional difficulties. Negative—One who deliberately plays on the emotions of others to get his or her own way and make other people look like the instigator of the problems.

Magickal Attributes: See Pegasus.

Arabian Buraq

The Arabs have a story of a magickal flying horse called Al Borak, Buraq, or Burak. This creature was the milk-white steed of Mohammed and could outdistance human sight in a single stride. It finally carried Mohammed to heaven from Jerusalem. It is said that the hoofmark of this magickal animal can still be seen at the place where it left the ground.

An ancient Persian miniature exists which portrays Buraq with a human head and peacock-feather tail. Buraq's face in this miniature looks like that of a female; however, tradition does not say anything about Mohammed's steed being female.

BURAQ

Working with the astral energies of Buraq can aid you in reaching new spiritual heights.

Psychological Attributes: Positive—A person who seeks higher spiritual paths in order to better his or her life. Negative—One who is cruel or abusive to those who are not of his or her religion.

Magickal Attributes: Reaching the Upperworld in meditation or trance.

Sleipnir

Norse-Germanic myths tell of a wonderful, mystical horse which belonged to the god Odhinn or Wodan. Sleipnir had eight legs, was a cloud-gray, and, although he did not have wings, could ride over water or in the air, and pull almost any weight. Sleipnir was a symbol of death and the journey into the Underworld.[3] He was the offspring of the malicious Loki and the giant stallion Svadilfari. When Balder was slain, Hermod rode to Hel on Sleipnir, easily jumping the surrounding wall of this Underworld realm.

The name Sleipnir comes from Old Norse and means "Slipper, Sliding One."[4] Skalds (bards) used the kenning "high-chested rope-Sleipnir" to mean the gallows on which human sacrifices were hung to Odhinn. In Old Norse, *drasil* meant both "horse" and "gallows tree."

Sleipnir ordinarily did not allow anyone but Odhinn to ride him. However, under special orders from this god, the great horse would carry humans on one-way trips to escape danger.

As the leader of the Wild Hunt, which ranged through the stormy night skies, Odhinn was also known as the Wild Huntsman. Leading his fierce host of warriors mounted on their cloud-gray horses, Odhinn swept through the forests, over the mountains, and through the skies above the villages, sometimes carrying away those who scoffed at them. The appearance of this wild band was said to herald plagues, war, and violence. Farmers left the last sheaf of grain in the field as fodder for Sleipnir and the other Hunt horses, so they would pass by without injuring the people.

In France, the leader of the Wild Hunt was known as the Grand Huntsman of Fontainebleau, also a sky-rider on a magickal steed. On the eve of the French revolution and on the night of the murder of Henry IV, people clearly heard the cries of these huntsmen and the whine of their dogs.

SLEIPNIR

In England, the Wild Huntsman has become known as Herne the Hunter, a strange antler-crowned figure who haunts Windsor Park. He also rides through the skies on stormy nights.

Christianity could not destroy the belief in the Wild Hunt, so religious leaders tried to explain it away by saying the Hunt was led by the Christian devil. They managed to eliminate the older references to the Huntsman and his magickal horse in the story of Dietrich of Bern, a Teutonic hero. (For more on this, see Chapter 14.)

Sleipnir is a mythological symbol of both the human fear of and natural attraction to the astral journey at the death of the body. Each time we go on a controlled astral journey, we are practicing for the last astral journey we will take in every lifetime.

This magickal horse can help you make astral contact with deceased friends, loved ones, and even distant ancestors. You can also call upon Sleipnir for help in facing your own mortality or the impending death of a loved one, or when you need guidance for facing your shadow-self.

Psychological Attributes: Positive—One who helps others find their highest spiritual paths. Negative—A person who enjoys persecuting, stalking, or hounding others.

Magickal Attributes: Journeying to the Underworld to visit great teachers of the past. Escaping danger; coming to terms with death as part of the life cycle.

Alsvidr and Arvakr

Alsvidr and Arvakr are the names of the two supernatural Norse horses which pull the Sun through the sky. In Old Norse, Alsvidr means "very quick," while Arvakr means "early awake."

In the *Gylfaginning*, Snorri Sturluson tells the story of why the gods placed these horses in the sky. A man named Mundilfari had two children so beautiful that he named his son Mani (Moon) and his daughter Sol (Sun). The gods thought Mundilfari was arrogant; they took the children and put them in the sky. They made the Sun out of a spark which flew up from Muspellheim, and they set Sol the task of driving the horses which pulled this illuminating body. These horses were Arvakr and Alsvidr. To keep these celestial horses cool, the gods fastened two bellows beneath their shoulders.

These Nordic Sun horses can help you find and follow the right physical or spiritual path.

Psychological Attributes: Positive—Having a positive attitude that you can reach your goals. Negative—Criticizing and belittling others because of jealousy.

Magickal Attributes: Keeping cool under stress and pressure.

Vivasvat

Hindu mythology tells of a great seven-headed Sun horse called Vivasvat. The Sun god married Saranya, the daughter of Tvashtar; through her, Vivasvat, in the form of a man, became first the father of twins: Yama, king of the dead, and his sister Yami. Saranya, however, fled from Vivasvat's terrible heat, shape-shifting into a mare and leaving behind a simulacrum of herself upon whom Vivasvat begat Manu. Realizing the deception, the Sun god formed himself into a stallion and begat upon the mare the Asvins, or horse-men.

This Hindu Sun horse with his seven heads symbolizes chakra work, a vital part of magickal endeavors.

Psychological Attributes: Positive—Being modest about your abilities and talents. Negative—Pushing yourself onto people who are uninterested in you.

Magickal Attributes: Enlightenment and shapeshifting.

VIVASVAT

Other Flying Horses

An eighth-century ivory plectrum from Japan shows a clear image of a horse-bird figure. This creature has only two legs with hooves, two wings, and a long feathery tail. The head is crowned with rising feathers.[5]

The story of the Faery Morgana tells of Papillon, a fire-breathing horse. It carried Ogier the Dane to Morgana's castle, and over one hundred years later returned him to the court of France. Ogier was astonished to discover that Charlemagne had been dead for many years and that Hugh Capet was king.

Psychological Attributes: Positive (Papillon)—Seeing the truth in situations and adjusting. Negative—Refusing to see the truth and insisting that everyone else is wrong.

Magickal Attributes: Traveling into the world of Faery during meditation.

ENDNOTES

1. E. A. Wallis Budge. *Dwellers on the Nile.*
2. Bellerophon could not have caught Pegasus if Athene had not told him how in a dream.
3. The Welsh had a horse-god with many of the same characteristics, whom they called Waelsi or Waels.
4. Rudolf Simak. *Dictionary of Northern Mythology.*
5. These feathers could possibly be identified as a single horn, although this is stretching identification to its limits.

5

Centaurs

The Centaur was known to various cultures in the Middle and Near East, but we are acquainted with this creature primarily through Greek lore. Centaurs were almost always portrayed as male, although there must have been females as well. The Bayeux Tapestry shows the figure of a female Centaur, along with a winged male Centaur.

In Crete, the Centaurs were said to be descendants of Leukippe, the White Mare Goddess. They may have been connected in some way with the same horse-masked priestesses of the Pirene fountain who honored Pegasus. The Greeks called these priestesses the "man-eating mares."

The Centaurs pictured in Greek art had the upper body, head, and arms of a man and the lower body and legs of a stallion. They were a wild, shaggy, ancient people, renowned for their wizardry, who primarily inhabited the mountainous regions of Arcadia and Thessaly in Greece. Although handsome in appearance, their character, more often than not, left much to be desired. There were two separate branches of the Centaur family; these were opposite in temperament.

There are several legends about the origin of Centaurs. Robert Graves tells about the two very different types of Centaurs and their creation. The man Ixion was the son of Phlegyas, the Lapith king. Eioneus, his future father-in-law, invited Ixion to a banquet, but Ixion repaid Eioneus by laying a fire-trap. Eioneus fell into the pit and was burned alive. Zeus, a scoundrel himself, took Ixion to Olympus and purified him of his sins. Ixion, however, had not changed; he immediately made plans to seduce Hera. Hera escaped by making an image of herself from a cloud. Ixion, too drunk to know the difference, took his pleasure with the cloud. The resulting child was Centaurus,[1] who later sired the horse-men on the Magnesian mares. Sometimes these Centaurs were called the Magnetes,[2] or "great ones," which comes from the name Magnesian. This branch of the Centaurs was like Cheiron and Pholus—wise and just.[3]

Hellenic myths say that the Centaur Cheiron[4] was the son of a god and was skilled in hunting, medicine, music, and divination. This particular Centaur was especially skilled in the use of medicinal herbs. One of Cheiron's semi-divine students was Asclepius, a god of healing and medicine. The wild, shaggy Greek Centaurs were considered to be great wizards, shape-shifters, and well-versed in occult lore. They taught their skills to the gods and special heroes.[5]

Since Centaurs often acted on behalf of Underworld deities, their images were sometimes put on Greek and Roman tombs and funeral monuments.

The second and more numerous branch of Centaurs were the children of Cronus and his wife, the beautiful sea nymph Philyra. A drunken, lecherous bunch, these Centaurs reveled in the free-flowing wine, orgies, and all-night celebrations of this deity. Any woman unfortunate enough to meet any of these Centaurs had to run for her honor. The Centaur Nessus was one of this type.

When Hercules was traveling with his wife Deianira, they came to a raging, flooded river. The water was too swift for Hercules to swim while carrying his wife. The Centaur Nessus appeared and offered to carry Deianira across if Hercules would swim by himself. The Greek hero swam across, only to look back and see the Centaur running away with his wife. Hercules shot the Centaur with a poisoned arrow and killed him. While Hercules was swimming back across the river,

CENTAUR

the dying Nessus told Deianira to dip one of Hercules' shirts in the Centaur's blood as a love charm. If the hero's love ever began to fail, she could renew it by having the hero wear the shirt. Deianira, believing that all Centaurs were wise and just, did as he said. Several years later, Hercules captured a beautiful woman named Iole and fell in love with her. Deianira sent him the blood-tainted shirt, which he immediately wore. The Centaur's blood burned Hercules' flesh and killed the hero.[6]

Other cultures also knew and recognized the Centaur. The Indo-Europeans may have brought the knowledge of this man-horse creature with them when they traveled through Greece. The area of central Asia had a belief in man-horse wizards also. Even Assyrian seals show the Centaur.

Centaur figures were known in the Kassite and Middle Assyrian, as well as the Babylonian Periods of civilization. Images of these creatures have been found on seals, sealings, and stamp-seals. The Centaurs of the Middle East, however, sometimes have scorpion tails. Often they are shown holding a bow or club and hunting other animals.

In English heraldry, the Centaur without a bow is almost unheard of, but the Centaur armed with drawn bow appears in the coats of arms of a few English and Scottish families, besides some on the Continent. The unarmed Centaur figure does appear in the heraldry of several Continental families. The most famous coat of arms bearing a Centaur belonged to King Stephen, who invaded England in 1135. However, Stephen's Centaurs are sometimes shown with the body of a lion instead of a horse. It was not until the Renaissance that the Centaur began to be used in heraldry.

Centaurs of all types represent the constant human struggle between the intellect and the emotions. Complete domination of emotions, however, is just as unbalanced as uncontrolled emotions. We need to strive for a balance, projecting our emotions when necessary, but not letting them rule us. By the same token, the intellect must never be in total control, either.

Psychological Attributes: Positive—A person who has learned to control the beast-side of human nature and apply the forces for good. Negative—The subconscious mind uncontrolled by the spirit. Complete domination by baser forces. Centaurs represent humans with their human heads and hands and the bodies of beasts. If a person resonates with the lecherous branch of the species, one can experience strong, often out-of-control, sexual feelings. Someone who is proud of his or her physical attributes and/or prowess and uses these traits to attract sexual partners.

Magickal Attributes: Healing magick, shape-shifting, music, the arts, divination. Inspiration for an artistic talent. Learning to control physical impulses and emotions; overcoming physical desires that are not good for you. The master-teacher Cheiron was considered to be the guardian and teacher of ancient secret doctrines. Call upon him specifically when in need of this information.

Sileni

Many people think that Sileni is just another word for Centaur, but this is not the case. Although the Sileni were also part horse, they were very different from the Centaurs. They had the tail and ears of a horse, but the rest of their form was that of a man. These creatures lived in Phrygia, but were known to the Greeks. They also followed Dionysus.

Silenus, the leader of the Sileni, was pictured as fat, bald, and snub-nosed. Although always drunk, he was full of wisdom and even taught Dionysus. Silenus could reveal the destiny of anyone, for he knew both the past and the future. Marsyas, who is usually called a Satyr, was really a Sileni.

Psychological Attributes: Positive—More of a human-controlled personality than that of the Centaur, but given to periodic (sometimes even calculated) outbursts of animalistic sexual ideas and activities. These ideas and activities can be positive if approved by your partner and limited to him or her. Negative—If you indulge yourself by foisting unwanted activities onto your partner or using these feelings as an excuse to bed-hop.

Magickal Attributes: To learn the past and future; destiny.

Asvins and Gandharvas

In the Hindu pantheon were the Asvins, or Aswins, and the Gandharvas, both connected with horses. The Vedic name Asvins means "the knights" or "the horsemen." However, these beings are able to assume any form they wish. They are portrayed as two golden or honey-colored males, young and handsome. Their personal names are sometimes given as Dasra and Nasatya. The name Nasatya is also used to indicate the pair.

One source says Nasatya comes from the Vedic root-word *nas,* meaning "to save," a reference to their duties as physicians to the gods and friends of the sick and unfortunate. According to Alain Danielou, however, Nasatya means "Inseparables."

The Asvins were Indian twin gods[7] whose horses pulled their three-wheeled golden chariot through the morning sky, preparing a path through the clouds for Ushas, the dawn goddess. Their chariot was made for them by the triad of Rhibus, sons of Sudhanvan (good archer). Their whips scattered the morning dew. At evening twilight, they took a similar ride through the heavens. Their loyalty belonged to the god Indra.

Hindu myths say that Vivasvat (the horse of the Sun) was their sire by the cloud goddess Saranyu, a nymph who changed herself into a mare. Surya, the Sun goddess and daughter of Savitri, was wife to both the Asvins.

The Asvins were considered to be the physicians of the gods, or healing deities. They were said to know all the secrets of plant and herb life. They were also protectors of love and marriage, old age, and the givers of honey.

The Asvins are similar to the Greek Dioskuroi (sons of Zeus), Kastor and Polydeukes, who also were never seen without their horses. The Greeks called the Dioskuroi *leukippoi,* meaning "having white steeds."

The Gandharvas were demi-gods who lived in the heaven of Indra. Their name means "the Fragrances." These beings are shown with a human torso and legs, but usually with a horse's head, although on occasion they wear a bird's head.

They are considered to be highly skilled horsemen. Deities of the air, rain, and rain clouds, the Gandharvas are connected with medicine, healing, and marriage, like the Asvins. However, they also deal with reincarnation, divine truths, and musical skills. Because of their supreme skill in music and musical knowledge, they are considered benevolent toward singers and musicians. They are also guardians of the sacred soma.

Sometimes the name Gandharvas is coupled with the name Apsaras. This is because they are the licentious mates of the Apsaras, aquatic and woodland nymphs. Even today the Gandharvas are portrayed in masquerades as phallic man-horses, representing the fecundity of Nature.

Psychological Attributes: Positive—If you resonate to the Asvins and Gandharvas as human-type beings who control their horse-beast aspects. Negative—If you identify with these beings as horse-men who spend their days occupied with sexual thoughts about the nymphs.

GANDHARVAS

Magickal Attributes: Asvins—Friends of the sick and unfortunate. Healing, plant and herb life, old age; protectors of love and marriage. Gandharvas—Rain, divine truth, healing, medicine, musical skills; connected with marriage and reincarnation. Guardians of the sacred initiation drink.

Aughisky

Yeats declared that this water-horse is the same as the Highland Each Uisge.[8] The Aughiska, or Aughisky [agh-iski], were once so common that they often left the sea to gallop over the sands or fields. This happened mostly in November. If anyone could get one of these water-horses away from the sands and sea and put a bridle and saddle on it, the Aughisky made a wonderful horse. However, one could never allow it so much as a glimpse of salt water, or it would race deep into the sea, carrying the rider with it. There, it devoured the rider. The untamed Aughisky were also said to devour cattle during their ventures ashore.

Psychological Attributes: If you find yourself fighting a losing battle to control runaway, and perhaps dangerous, emotions of all kinds, you have serious work to do on your personality. You are allowing the Aughisky to project its negative power through you. This is a very negative type of magickal beast.

Magickal Attributes: Not recommended except by the most accomplished magicians. If the Aughisky sees even a hint of uncontrolled emotion (water), it will be completely out of your control. Being able to control an unpleasant situation without emotion.

Cabyll Ushtey

Another water-horse known in the Isle of Man was the Cabyll Ushtey. This creature was a pale gray color. It was as dangerous and liked human flesh as much as the Highland Each Uisge. There are few tales recorded about the Cabyll Ushtey. One tale tells of one such creature who visited Kerroo Clough on the Dark River for a period of time before disappearing.

Psychological Attributes: A viciousness which delights in destroying others. Humans who have these traits most definitely need counseling. Abusers and some murderers fall into this category.

Magickal Attributes: Not recommended.

Each Uisge

This Highland water-horse is the fiercest and most dangerous of all the water-horses, with the Cabyll Ushtey a close second. The Each Uisge [ech-ooshkya] haunts the sea and lochs, while the milder Highland Kelpie stays in running water. The Each Uisge usually appears as a sleek horse which will offer to be ridden; however, it has also been known to appear as a giant bird or a handsome young man. In its horse form, if a human mounts it, he or she is "stuck"— the person is helpless and unable to dismount. The Each Uisge then will race straight into the lake with the rider, where it devours all but the liver.

The Glastyn or Glashtin from the Isle of Man is similar to the Each Uisge. When this being appears in human form, it is usually as a handsome, dark man with curly hair and flashing eyes. However, his delicate ears look like those of a horse.

Psychological Attributes: Anyone who appears gentle until he or she gets you emotionally attached, then sets about deliberately "eating up" your life, is expressing traits of the Each Uisge. Psychic vampires who masquerade as friends, then "suck" off your energy, fall into this category.

Magickal Attributes: Not recommended; very dangerous.

Irish Phouka

The Irish Phouka [pooka] was a Faery entity with a human-like form that could take the shape of a horse, thus making it a type of Centaur. A number of Irish places still have names connected with the Phouka: Puckstown, Puck Fair, Pooka's Ford.[9] A falls on the Liffey River near Ballymore Eustace is called Pool-a-Phooka (The Pooka's Hole); in County Cork are the ruins of the castle Carrig-a-Phooka (The Pooka's Rock), while not far from Dublin is another old castle named Puck's Castle. The Irish occasionally still see the Phouka in remote, lonely spots, especially bogs and swamps. They believe that seeing a Phouka is a bad omen. Many a person who was foolish enough to mount the Irish Phouka had a terrifying ride before he or she was allowed to dismount.

Psychological Attributes: This is a person who thinks his or her practical jokes, which actually humiliate and belittle others, are funny.

Magickal Attributes: The appearance of the Phouka signals a coming period of "bad" luck. This ordinarily applies to events, great or small, which may affect your personal life. An accomplished magician can use the Phouka to return

PHOUKA

humorless energy to a practical joker. Learning to see the true person behind the mask. Not recommended except for skilled magicians.

Kelpies

In Scotland dwells a creature known as a Kelpie; in Cornwall it is called a Shoney. This is a Faery spirit who lives in water. Sometimes it can assume the shape of a human or even a seal, but more often it reveals itself as a white horse with a mane like the foam on waves. A clue to the presence of Kelpies in nearby water is their loud wailing just before a storm.

When in human-like form, the Kelpie emerges from the water looking like a hairy semi-human with seaweed hair. It hides in the bushes waiting for a passing horseman. Leaping up behind the unsuspecting person, the Kelpie throws its hairy arms around the victim, crushing the rider until he or she loses control of the horse. The frightened horse will be chased along the banks until the Kelpie tires of the game and leaps back into the water.

KELPIE

In its other form, the Kelpie appears along the river bank as a magnificent young horse wearing a bridle. Any human foolish enough to mount the Kelpie is immediately taken into the deepest part of the water and nearly drowned before he or she can get off.

A person who is wise to the habits of Kelpies can carry an ordinary bridle along on a journey. If the person spots a horse-formed Kelpie, he or she can mount it, then quickly substitute the ordinary bridle for the one the Kelpie is wearing. If this switch is successful, the Kelpie can be made to work for the human. Tradition says, however, that a captured Kelpie should not be overworked or kept too long, lest it curse the human and all his or her descendants.

Some people believe that the Kelpie eats humans. However, this habit belongs to another of the Scottish water-horses, not the Kelpie. The flesh-eating water-horses were called Ech-Ushkya and lived in the lochs. They would appear in the form of small ponies along the banks. As soon as a human mounted the Ech-Ushkya, the rider would find that he or she could not dismount. The water-horse would dash into the deepest part of the loch, dragging its victim underwater. Sometimes a portion of the body would float to the surface later.

Psychological Attributes: A person who plays with the emotions of others but does not want to keep them attached and dependent. Or, a person who loves the more harmful type of practical joke.

Magickal Attributes: Not recommended, except by experienced magicians. Dealing with troubled emotions.

Noggle

People of the Shetland Islands know a creature called the Noggle (Nuggle or Nygel). When it appeared, always near water, it resembled a small gray horse with bridle and saddle, its tail curled up over its back. It was ordinarily not dangerous to humans but did have two mischievous habits. If a mill was running at night, the Noggle would stop the wheel. If anyone mounted the Noggle, it would dash into the water, rider and all. When it rose from the water, it would vanish in a blue flame. Sometimes people called it a Shoopiltie, a name it shared with the Mer-People.

Psychological Attributes: A person who loves to get another person more than a little interested or attracted to him or herself, a project, or an activity, then dump or exclude the other person without explanation.

Magickal Attributes: An accomplished magician can use the Noggle to turn the negative habits of a person who likes to collect "conquests" back upon the troublemaker.

NOGGLE

Nokke

In Denmark, legends tell of the Nokke or Neck, a water spirit who can live in both fresh and salt water. Always male, the Nokke has a human head, chest, and arms, but a horse-like body under the water. The face looks like that of a handsome young man, with golden ringlets and a red cap. He likes to sit on the water during warm summer nights, playing his gold harp. Sometimes the Nokke shape-shifts into an old bearded man and sits on the sea cliffs, wringing out his beard. There are stories of Nokkes falling in love with human women; the creature is always very polite and attentive, but still dangerous, as he takes the object of his love back into the water with him, never to be seen again.

As with other Water-Folk, the Nokke can be repelled by metal, especially steel or iron. Fishermen and those who must travel on water protect themselves against the Nokke by putting a knife or nail in the bottom of the boat.

Psychological Attributes: An attractive, and often agreeable-appearing human, who will fall in love with another person, then separate that person from his or her former life and activities as much as possible. This is done to gain control and give a feeling of power.

Magickal Attributes: Not recommended.

ENDNOTES

1. Called "unblest by the Graces" because he was so evil.
2. John Cuthbert Lawson. *Modern Greek Folklore & Ancient Greek Religion.*
3. Robert Graves. *Greek Myths.*
4. Pliny called Cheiron the most just of the Centaurs and "the Beast Divine."
5. Robert Graves. *The White Goddess.*
6. I find it difficult to believe that any woman was gullible enough to believe this Centaur's word after just being abducted by him. It is more likely that Deianira knew exactly what the Centaur's blood would do. Since Hercules was known for his roving eye, his wife probably kept the shirt to use if he got out of hand and decided to leave her for another woman.
7. The Rig Veda mentions that these horse-gods were twins.
8. Yeats. *Irish Fairy & Folk Tales.*
9. Elizabeth Pepper and John Wilcock. *Magical & Mystical Sites.*

6

Satyrs and Fauns

Although many people equate Fauns with Satyrs, these two classes of beings have vastly different temperaments and legends. Satyrs, even more than Centaurs, symbolize the human sexual drive overruling the intellect. Humans often speak of "being in love" when they mean "being in lust." We let our hormones lead us into relationships better avoided. When our intellect finally does get its say, usually after we have been thoroughly used and abused in some manner, we are embarrassed that we were so foolish.

Fauns, on the other hand, represent the normal use of sexual emotions influenced by both hormones and the intellect. In this aspect, humans do not rush into relationships, but give them time to grow naturally. Sex, instead of being the only common bond, becomes a by-product of a deep friendship.

51

Satyrs

The Greek Satyrs were horned deities of wild Nature who followed the gods Pan, Dionysus, and Bacchus. They had the body, arms, and sex organs of men combined with the slanted eyes, flat noses, pointed ears, legs, cloven hooves, small horns, and tails of goats. Their bodies were mostly covered with coarse, curly hair; their faces were more like those of monkeys than humans, with a flat or snub nose and a low forehead. They loved music, dancing, human women, wood Nymphs, and wine. It was said that they perpetuated their race by raping wood Nymphs; water Nymphs were safe because the Satyrs were afraid of water. They were extremely malicious mischief-makers at times, scattering flocks of sheep and terrifying lone travelers. They reveled in drunken vandalism, which was often blamed on humans.

Hesiod wrote that Satyrs were basically a lazy, useless race of creatures who only liked to indulge their personal pleasures. Some myths say they were brothers of the wood Nymphs and the Curetes.[1] Nonnus wrote that Satyrs were related to the Centaurs.

Satyrs were most common in the deep woods where they liked to dance to the music of their flutes, called syrinxes. Their special dance was known as the *sikinnis,* which required goat-like agility.

Like the god Dionysus, the Satyrs were connected with the ivy crown, the *thyrsos* (wand), grapes, the cornucopia, and snakes. In his chthonic aspect, Dionysus was known as Melanaigis (a name which came from his wearing a black goatskin) and blew on a horn-trumpet. This aspect of Dionysus was honored at the oldest Athenian religious festival, the Apaturia (Feast of Common Relationship). The Maenads, human women who took part in the orgies of Dionysus, willingly gave themselves sexually to the Satyrs.

The Roman Satyrs were sometimes pictured with goat feet, but other times as young human male companions of Bacchus. In their human-like form, they had pointed ears and little horns on their heads, dressed in panther skins, and carried flutes. The Roman Satyrs were considered much milder and less aggressive in forcing their sexual attentions on women.

The Roman Sileni were similar in temperament to the Roman Satyrs, but were described as having the shapes of young men with the ears and tail of a horse. (See Chapter 5.)

There are rare records of sightings of Satyrs. St. Jerome wrote that during the reign of Constantine, a Satyr was captured alive. It

SATYR CAUSING TROUBLE

had a human form but with the horns and feet of a goat. It was exhibited to the people of Greece until it died; then the creature was preserved in salt and taken to the Emperor Constantine so that he could testify to its existence.[2]

Aldrovandus, a medieval writer, stated that there were many Satyrs living in Ireland.

Psychological Attributes: A person whose existence revolves around parties, good times, sexual encounters, and drinking. One who will push his or her sexual attentions on another. Rapists fall into this category, as do those who prey on children and young adults.

Magickal Attributes: Music, dancing, lovemaking. Dealing with lustful and untamed emotions. Learning to handle obnoxious, sexualminded people. Use absolutely no drugs, alcohol, or stimulants when calling upon the Satyrs.

Fauns

The Romans also knew another milder version of the Satyr called a Faun. A later description says these woodland spirits were half-man, half-goat, with twisted ram-horns,[3] pointed ears, and a goat tail.

However, earlier descriptions portray them as having the legs, tail, and ears of a deer with the body and face of a young man; the torso and arms were smooth-skinned, the legs smooth-haired. As companions of the god Faunus (consort of the goddess Fauna), Fauns lived in the wild forests. Gentle creatures, they enticed their human companions into their woodland revels, rather than chasing them down like the Satyrs did. It was not unusual to see a band of Nymphs and Fauns dancing together. The music made by the Fauns sometimes enticed human females to go out at night to dance naked in the moonlight.

Faunus, also known as Lupercus, was an Italian god of the countryside. The Romans identified him with the Greek Pan, but Faunus was really much different. He invented the shawm, a kind of flute; the Fauns were expert players of this instrument. Sometimes said to be the grandson of Saturn, sometimes a descendant of Mars, Faunus was considered a god of prophecy. At one time the Isle of Capri was dedicated to this goat god.

The native Italian woodland god Silvanus was popular in Roman Britain. He was sometimes called Callirius (Woodland King). In Britain he was shown with hammers, pots, and a billhook, a tool of the native wood-warden. He was associated with stags.

A similar woodland deity, the Wild Herdsman, is well-known through Welsh myths such as Culhwch and Olwen and the Lady of the Fountain. In these stories he appears as a black giant with a huge club. He is the guardian of the forest animals, an instructor in wisdom, and the genius of the primal forest. One of his earlier Celtic names was Cernunnos ("Horned One").

Psychological Attributes: Positive—A love for Nature and everything in it. Negative—Taking a delight in causing terror in others; being caught up in seeing how many sexual partners one can have.

FAUN

Magickal Attributes: Agriculture, flocks, bees, fishing, gardens and orchards, animals, fertility, Nature, woodlands, music, dance, medicine, soothsaying. Gentleness in relationships.

English Pooka and Puck

The English Puca was a woodland Faery-type creature who had a human-like form. The name Puca produced the words "spook" and "Puck."[4] Pouk-ledden was a common term, meaning someone who had wandered off the path had been led astray by Puck. Although mischievous, the English Puca, sometimes called a Pooka, is not a lascivious creature.

In Britain proper this entity became known as Puck, a woodland entity who caused all kinds of mischief.[5] Puck was a harmless sprite, whose name evolved into the word "puckish," meaning mischievous. Ayto says the name and nature of Puck later was given to Robin Good-fellow.[6] A shape-shifter, Puck liked to help humans as long as they appreciated and acknowledged his existence. However, he disliked and tended to persecute those who scorned their lovers.

KORNBOKE (POOKA)

Puck, who looked a bit like a Pixie with his pointed ears, liked to wear a close-fitting suit of green. A friend of all Faeries, he played on a willow twig flute for their dances in the moonlight. He preferred foxes, rabbits, squirrels, and other wild creatures to the domesticated ones favored by Pan. However, Puck took an interest in and helped all plants and creatures of the forests and fields.

The Pwca (pooka) of Wales is a version of the

English Puck. Cwm Pwca is said to be one of his favorite places. The Pwca of Wales are very ugly, ill-tempered, and often quarrel among themselves. Unlike other Pookas, the Pwca will come down a chimney into a human home. The Welsh say that Shakespeare based his Puck on their Pwca.

In Scandinavian and German countries the Pooka are known as the Kornbockes; they are said to have goat-bodies, probably resembling Fauns. They will help grow grain and corn, but will steal or spoil it if they get a chance.

In Old German Puck is known as Putz or Butz, while in Iceland he is called Puki and is considered to be an evil spirit.

Psychological Attributes: Positive—One who has a wry, but harmless, sense of humor; one who feels especially close to the Earth and its creatures. Negative—One who likes to play tricks on others, but never takes responsibility if things go wrong.

Magickal Attributes: The flute, untamed wild animals, dance and music. Punishment of wandering lovers. Call upon Puck to learn gentle humor. He is mischievous but helpful.

Jack in the Green

The English countryside also had another type of woodland entities known as the Green Men. These Faery-like creatures had green human forms and wore scanty outfits made of leaves. Non-threatening beings, unless you were a woodcutter or game-keeper, the Green Men cared for the trees in the dense forests. The Green Men were seldom seen by the average human.

Another form of the Green Man was the Celtic Cernunnos, god of the woodlands, animals, and fertility. In Old Welsh his name was Arddhu (the Dark One), Atho, or the Horned God.

Jack in the Green is a legendary woodland spirit of Britain. Like the Woodwose, he was guardian of the woodlands or greenwoods. He is often shown on roof-bosses, peering through leaves in church carvings.

In both Scotland and Cornwall are short, thin male beings known as the Brown Men or Moor Men. They have coppery-red hair and dress in brown moorland foliage to avoid detection. Although they do not dislike humans, they avoid them whenever possible. Their task seems to be to protect and nurture animal life on the moors.

The Oak Men live in Germany and parts of Scandinavia where they guard groves of sacred oak trees. Although they are not friendly toward humans, they make no effort to harm them.

Psychological Attributes: Positive—One who is drawn to protect the woodlands. Negative—One who is fanatical about forest protection, even to the detriment of fellow humans.

Magickal Attributes: Protect woodlands and trees, especially oak trees; protect wild animals.

Pan

Pan was known to the Greeks as the "Little God," the Horned God of Nature, or the Goat-Foot God; he originated in Arcadia and was a frequent companion of the god Dionysus. The word "panoply," meaning elaborate religious ceremonies, may have originated with his name.

Pan was one of the oldest Greek deities and the Positive Life Force of the World. He had a human-shaped body, head, and arms with the hooves, legs, small horns, and long ears of a large goat. He played enticing, beguiling music on his syrinx or pan-pipes. However, he knew the power of magickal words and used his voice to beguile or command humans. Mythology says Pan coupled with all the Maenads, as well as Athene, Penelope, and Selene.[7]

In his gentler aspect, Pan symbolized the woodlands and the wild creatures, healing, gardening, plants and animals, music and dancing, soothsaying, and lovemaking. Unlike the Satyrs, Pan helped shepherds and huntsmen, unless they offended him.

However, he had a dark side in which he caused the wild and unreasoning terror sometimes experienced by people in lonely woodlands and mountains. His magick and terrible cry scattered his enemies, filling them with heart-pounding terror. From this behavior comes our word "panic." His sacred drama of death and resurrection gave birth to the original Greek "tragedy" (the Greek word *tragoidos* meant "goat song"[8]).

The Greeks identified the Egyptian deity Amen-Ra with Pan and called Amen-Ra's holy city of Chemnis Panopolis, "city of Pan."

PAN

Ancient Greek writers said that Panopolis was the home of Pan and many Satyrs.[10] The Satyrs portrayed in Roman art have the same type of twisted, horizontal ram's horns as the Egyptian god.

Psychological Attributes: Positive—Pan represents the procreative energies. Therefore, a person showing Pan traits would use his or her energies and powers of creation for good. Negative—A person who uses his or her energies to create fear in others.

Magickal Attributes: Music, magick words, woodlands and wild creatures, healing, gardening, herbs, dance, soothsaying, lovemaking. Overcoming barriers in relationships. Also creating unreasonable terror; this is appropriate only against abusers, rapists, and murderers.

The Urisk

In Scotland lives a strange little Brownie known as the Urisk or Uruisg. These solitary creatures were half-human, half-goat. Usually they lived around lonely pools, but sometimes sought human company. Although one of their tricks was to follow and terrify travelers at night, they sometimes came to live near a house. They were considered lucky as they would help with the farm work and herd cows. Ordinarily each Urisk lived alone, but gathered together on certain occasions. Although no one is clear on when these meetings took place, the Urisk probably met on the Equinoxes, Solstices, and the other four Pagan festivals, as did the Faeries and other Earth beings.

Psychological Attributes: Positive—A person who has a unique rapport with animals. Negative—One who delights in frightening others.

Magickal Attributes: Very lucky. As with Pan, call upon the Urisk to heal animals and help in the garden.

The Woodland Leshy

Sometimes the Slavic-Russian woodland spirits known as the Leshy (Leshi) were said to resemble the Satyrs, with human bodies and the horns, ears, and legs of a goat. This may be one branch of the Leshy, since the other members of this species primarily haunt the water and areas near it. These woodland Leshy are forest guardians, most active at dusk and dawn during the spring and summer. They never physically harm humans, but enjoy getting them lost in the thick underbrush and trees.

The word Leshy (or Leshi) describes both the Slavic Lord of the Forests and a multitude of woodland spirits who inhabit the Baltic forests. Some are dangerous, evil creatures, while others are simply mischievous. Their presence, however, can be felt by humans whenever these creatures are near. Foresters and others who are familiar with the forests say that the Leshy are extremely thin creatures with blue skin and green hair and eyes.

The Leshy prefer to live in the deep sections of the forest. They resent intruders to what they consider as their domain and will try to lead the travelers astray. During the winter, when snow is on the ground, the Leshy will wipe out footprints so the trail cannot be retraced. During

LESHY

other seasons, they will cause a sense of bewilderment in the traveler's mind so he or she wanders deeper and deeper into the forest, becoming hopelessly lost.

Foresters say you always know when the Leshy are trailing you. The trees feel as if they are moving and hemming you in; you get a prickly sensation of being watched. But however fast you turn around, you will never see the Leshy, for they can move faster than you can. The only way to throw them off your trail is to put your shoes on the wrong feet and your clothes on backward. This seems to confuse the Leshy to such a degree that their spell is broken, and you can escape.

Psychological Attributes: One who likes to deliberately, or even subconsciously, give wrong information to others as a joke; this person also likes to give bad advice just to see if you will follow it and mess up your life. Many humans who give this "bad advice" do so with ulterior motives: to have control over you or to see you fail.

Magickal Attributes: Dangerous. Help in protecting forests and trees.

WOODWOSE

Woodwose

Another branch of British woodland beings were the Woodwose, or Wild Men of the Woods. They were also called the Wooser or Ooser. They inhabited and guarded the wild woods. Unlike the Green Men who were covered in leaves, the Woodwose was covered with hair or long fur and wore no clothes. The literature of the sixteenth and seventeenth centuries has a few mentions of these entities but very little to say about them. In medieval times, their features were used on masks. In East Anglia especially, carvings of the Woodwose can still be seen in churches.

Psychological Attributes: Positive—A person who can live within an ordinary social frame, but still stand apart if necessary. Negative— One who withdraws from society, such as an extreme and fanatical survivalist.

Magickal Attributes: Healing and protecting really wild woodlands.

ENDNOTES

1. The Curetes were the protectors of the baby Zeus on Crete. The Greeks sometimes called them Gegeneis (children of the Earth) or Imbrogeneis (children of the rain). Mythology speaks of them as half-warrior, half-priest or priestess. They appear to have been devoted to Hera in later legends.

2. J.J. Bachofen. *Myth, Religion and Mother Right.* Edited by Joseph Campbell. Translated by Ralph Manheim. Princeton, NJ: Princeton University Press, 1973.

3. Manly Hall. *The Secret Teachings of All Ages.*

4. A Roman goblet shows a Faun's head: bearded male-like face; long, downward hanging ears; two horns joined at the top of the head and pointing outward.

5. Stephen Potter and Laurens Sargeant. *Pedigree.*

6. The Christians tried to make Puck and many other Faery creatures into their devil, or at least his minions.

7. John Ayto. *Arcade Dictionary of Word Origins.* Some writers say that Robin Goodfellow looks more like a Faun or Satyr than a human. He likes to play woodland pipes while he dances, and is a great friend of all woodland animals. Tradition says he had a Faery father and a human mother.

8. Robert Graves. *The White Goddess.*

9. Wildred Funk. *Word Origins & Their Romantic Stories.*

10. E. A. Wallis Budge. *Gods of the Egyptians.*

7

Gigantic Birds 1

There are a number of gigantic birds listed in the world's mythologies: some of them friendly to humans, some of them not. They were all of symbolic importance to ancient cultures. The Phoenix is, by far, the best-known of these great birds.

Phoenix

The Phoenix is known in various forms and by various names throughout the Middle and Far East, the Mediterranean, and Europe, as a symbol of resurrection. The name Phoenix may have come from the Greek *phoinix* and may be related to *phoinos* (blood-red). Although it was an enormous bird, it had certain characteristics of the eagle, pheasant, and the peacock.

The earliest known Greek reference to the Phoenix was by Hesiod in the eighth century B.C.E. Such Greek and Roman writers as Tacitus, Ovid, Pliny, Herodotus, and Hesiod referred to the Phoenix either as the Arabian Bird or the Egyptian Bird. An extremely gentle creature, it was said to weep tears of incense, while its blood was balsam.

There are two ancient records of first-hand sightings of a Phoenix: one by Pliny, who saw one exhibited in the Roman Forum during the reign of the Emperor Claudius; another by Clemont in the first century C.E.

The Phoenix was a graceful bird, with brilliant plumage and a distinctive tuft of feathers at the back of its head. There are at least three different descriptions of the plumage colors of the Phoenix. One says that the head, breast, and back are scarlet or reddish-gold, and the iridescent wings are many colors. Its feet are a Tyrian purple hue, while its eyes are sea-blue. Another says the body is plum-colored with a scarlet back and wing feathers, a golden head, and a long tail of rose and azure. The third description states that the Phoenix is a royal purple with a golden neck and head. It is possible that these descriptions are of the Phoenix in various stages of its life.

Tradition says that the Phoenix fed only on air, harming no other creature. It lived a solitary life in a far-away land, coming to human-inhabited land only when it was ready to die. The length of a Phoenix's life differs from ancient writer to writer; most believed that it lived for a thousand years.[1]

When the Phoenix knew its time had come, it flew to Arabia where it gathered myrrh, laudanum, nard, and cassia. Carrying a great load of these fragrances in its wings, the Phoenix flew on to Phoenicia. There, it chose the tallest palm tree and built a nest in it from the essences it had brought. At the next dawn, the great bird faced the rising Sun and sang in a beautiful voice. The heat of the Sun ignited the fragrant spices, and the Phoenix died in its own funeral pyre.

After nine days, a fledgling Phoenix rose out of the ashes. A few days later, when its wings were strong enough, the young Phoenix gathered the ashes of its parent and flew with them to Heliopolis in Egypt. Thousands of ordinary birds accompanied it on its journey. There, the new Phoenix put the ashes of its parent on the altar in the Sun temple. Then it flew toward the east and its distant home.

Other writers of the Phoenix story disagree on several points. Some said that instead of flying to Phoenicia with its spices, the

Phoenix flew directly to the temple at Heliopolis and built its funeral pyre on the altar there. Others believed that the priest of the Sun temple gathered the spices and prepared the nest for the Phoenix. A few writers recorded that the Phoenix did not rise straight from the ashes, but rather spent three days in a worm-like form before turning into the glorious Phoenix.

The Phoenix never died permanently. Legend says it existed when the universe was created and that it knows secrets of life and reincarnation that even the deities do not know.

Humans are fascinated by the sweet song of the Phoenix, and the bird is friendly to humans, although it seldom concerns itself with human affairs.

A similar mythological Egyptian bird was the Bennu, a heron-like bird. The Bennu was born in a spice-lined nest in a sycamore tree. It too made its own funeral pyre in which it died. Its first flight, after being reborn, was accompanied by thousands of ordinary birds. In fact, "Bennu" in Egyptian and "Phoenix" in Greek both mean "date palm." The bennu was sacred to Osiris and Ra, and a symbol of the Sun and resurrection.[2] It also represented the morning star.[3]

The Egyptian Phoenix was called the "Lord of jubilees," and was considered to be the *ba* (spirit) of the Sun god Ra. At one point in the Book of the Dead, the deceased says, "I have gone forth as a Phoenix." In Heliopolis, the Bennu was said to live in the *benben-stone* (obelisk) or in the sacred willow.

Queen Elizabeth I had a Phoenix engraved on her medals; Mary Queen of Scots also used the same emblem. Jane Seymour, who died giving birth to Edward VI, had a Phoenix crest, which her son later used.

In Mesopotamian art, the Phoenix may have been symbolized by the horned and winged solar disk.[4] Ancient bas-reliefs show this winged disk also having the tail-feathers, legs, and claws of a bird. Often this winged disk also had horns. The winged disk of Ahura Mazdah on a relief at Persepolis distinctly shows this disk with tail-feathers and bird's legs and feet.

Alchemists used the Phoenix to symbolize the color red and the successful end of a process, while medieval Hermeticists used the Phoenix as a symbol of alchemical transmutation. The word Phoenix was also used to identify one of the secret alchemical formulae.

The ancient Mysteries used the sign of the Phoenix to symbolize the immortality of the human soul and the great truths of esoteric philosophies revealed only through special initiations. In some ancient Mystery Schools, accepted initiates were referred to as Phoenixes, or those who had been "born again."

The Phoenix is a symbol of human hope. Throughout each lifetime, we encounter distressing and painful events which beat us down emotionally, physically, and/or mentally. When we gather our energies and rise from the "ashes" of these events, we become like the Phoenix. We also become Phoenix-like when we rebuild our spiritual lives after devastating and emotionally draining situations.

Psychological Attributes: The ability to overcome every partial death (change) which we must suffer in life. Rising out of the ashes of an old, devastating way of existence with the energy and knowledge needed to build a better life.

Magickal Attributes: Rebirth, renewal, spiritual growth. Call upon the Phoenix for strength and renewing energy when facing or undergoing trials in life.

Feng Huang

In China, the Phoenix was called the Feng Huang or Red Bird. It was one of the four spiritual animals, the special emblem of the empress, and the emperor of all birds. The Feng Huang was said to be similar to the Unicorn (Ch'i-lin) and often accompanied it. Feng designated the male bird, Huang the female. As with the Ch'i-lin, to speak of the species, one must say the Feng Huang. It is a very beautiful bird, its coloring like a combination of the pheasant and the peacock, but with a curling tail, curved beak, and long claws. Legend says that the Chinese musical scale came from the song of this Phoenix.

Chief among all the birds, the plumage of the Feng Huang is said to represent one of the basic five cardinal virtues. The devotion between the Feng and the Huang is so great that the Phoenix became a Chinese symbol of everlasting love. Stories say that the Phoenix lives only in the Vermilion Hills, that borderland between worlds, and that it draws the chariot of the immortal Jade Emperor. Like the Chinese Unicorn, appearances of the Feng Huang have always been rare; there have been no sightings for centuries. Legend says that the Feng Huang will only reappear when China is once more at peace.

FENG HUANG

The Feng Huang trait of everlasting love can be between friends, family, and/or lovers. It is a relationship in which each person balances and complements the other.

Psychological Attributes: Positive—One who acknowledges and develops the feminine side of his or her spiritual nature. Negative—One who denies and suppresses the feminine side of his or her spiritual nature.

Magickal Attributes: Music; everlasting love.

Japanese Ho-Ho

The Japanese know of a bird resembling the Feng Huang, with many characteristics of the Phoenix. It is called the Ho-Ho, possibly a name derived from its strange call. A solar symbol, this bird is said to live in the Japanese equivalent of heaven and only on rare occasions makes an appearance on Earth, always on a special errand, such as announcement of the beginning of a new era. The royal family, especially the empress, used the Ho-Ho as an emblem; its picture is often found on ancient bronzes and in paintings.

One delightful tale of the Ho-Ho tells of a young girl named Saijosen. Her skill at embroidery was so great that her creations seemed like living creatures captured on silk. One morning as she sat at her work, she suddenly noticed an elderly man beside her. He pointed to a blank portion of the silk and told her to embroider a pair of Ho-Ho birds there, which she did. It took her nearly all day to complete the design. When the light of the setting sun touched the wings of the embroidered birds, they came alive and stepped down from the cloth. The elderly man mounted one Ho-Ho, Saijosen the other, and they flew away to the land of the immortals.

The Ho-Ho represents the risk in relationships of both people not growing in the same direction or at the same rate. This applies especially in the areas of spirituality. If the relationship is balanced and in harmony, then both people will travel together. If one refuses to grow or grows in another direction, then there should be a parting of the ways.

Psychological Attributes: Positive—A person who strives toward perfection in a talent but keeps life balanced. Negative—One who is a fanatical perfectionist.

Magickal Attributes: Seldom can be summoned; appears when sent by the gods on a special errand.

Firebird

In Russia, there are old stories of the magickal and beautiful Firebird. Igor Stravinsky wrote the Firebird Suite to tell this story through music and ballet.

A young prince named Ivan was hunting deep in an enchanted forest when he came upon a strange high wall with a golden gate. As he looked through the gate, he saw a magickal Firebird, whose appearance changed back and forth between a bird and a woman. In her bird-form, she had feathers like flames, a beak and claws of gold, eyes like rubies, and long streamers of tail-feathers.

Not wishing to harm the Firebird, Ivan crept through the gate and trapped her in a net. Immediately, the brightness of the Firebird began to fade, for she could not live in captivity. Ivan felt sorry for her and let her go. In thanks, the Firebird dropped one of her feathers as she flew away. The magickal bird told the prince that he need only wave the feather three times when he needed her, and she would come to help him.

Ivan slipped the feather into his vest and went on to explore the garden. He found many strange stone statues, all with looks of horror on their faces. Soon he discovered a princess and her maidens trapped in the garden by an evil wizard named Kastchei. As the princess Elena warned Ivan to flee for his life, the garden wall suddenly grew as high as the clouds. The wizard arrived in a dark storm cloud. His appearance shifted between that of a tall, thin man dressed in swirling black robes and a skeleton with black bones and eyes like cold black fire.

Elena warned Ivan that he must avoid the wizard's touch or he would be turned into stone like all the others who came to rescue her. Kastchei called up a whirlwind which spit out horrible monsters that attacked the prince. Ivan pulled out the golden feather from his vest and waved it three times in the air. The Firebird suddenly appeared, casting a golden light around the prince and putting the monsters into a deep sleep.

Following the Firebird's advice, Ivan and the princess went to a great oak tree near a well. There they found a copper key which

FIREBIRD

would open the hiding place inside the wizard's palace which held the means of the wizard's death. Elena also took a pitcher of well water with her.

At the copper door to the palace was a three-headed Dragon; when Elena sprinkled it with the water, it fell asleep. Inside, Ivan opened a copper casket with the copper key and took out a little silver key. At a silver door was a six-headed Dragon which the princess also sprinkled with the water, causing it to fall asleep. The silver casket inside this room held a golden key. When they reached the golden door they found it guarded by a twelve-headed Dragon. This time the water did not put the creature to sleep until Ivan dipped the Firebird feather into it.

Elena opened the golden casket only to see a duck emerge and fly quickly toward a high window. Ivan immediately shot the duck with one of his arrows. The creature turned into a crystal egg, which Ivan caught.

Once more the Firebird appeared, followed by Kastchei. The wizard changed himself into a deadly whirlwind to kill the prince, but Ivan smashed the egg on the floor. The wizard turned into black ashes.

When Ivan and Elena returned to the garden, they found the gates open and all the statues transformed into living humans. The wizard's spell was broken at last. Promising to come if ever the prince and princess needed her, the Firebird flew off toward the east.

Psychological Attributes: One who has learned to listen to inner intuitive messages and act upon them with common sense.

Magickal Attributes: Defeat evil and controlling people.

Endnotes

1. Various numbers have been given for the length of a Phoenix's life: 350, 500, 1000, 1460, 7006, and 12,954 years. The figure of 1460 comes from the Egyptian Sothic cycle of calendar measurement, based on the position of the Dog Star Sirius.

2. E. A. Wallis Budge. *Gods of the Egyptians.*

3. Ibid.

4. Count Goblet d'Alviella. *Migration of Symbols.*

8

Gigantic Birds 11

Gigantic sky-birds, besides the Phoenix, were known in many cultures, especially in the Middle and Far East. The Persians had the Simurgh, the Arabs the Ruhk, and the Chinese the Fei Lien. The divine White Eagle of Zeus watched over the Two Gates of the World. These creatures were so huge they could blot out the Sun and darken the sky. Like the Phoenix, these giant birds held symbolic importance.

Arabian Ruhk and the Anka

The Ruhk (sometimes spelled Roc), described in the Arabian Nights stories, was said to be a gigantic bird. When it flew, it blotted out the Sun; it fed elephants to its young. Its egg was as large as 148 hen's eggs and looked like the dome of a mosque. Each feather was as large as a palm frond. Its wings

71

RUHK

created wind storms and lightning. Some parts of Arabic tradition say the Ruhk never landed on Earth, except on Mount Qaf, which the Arabs considered to be the axis mundi; other Arabian myths mention it landing in various isolated places. The Rook in chess was originally the Ruhk.

Ruhks were said to live on certain islands in the Indian Ocean. Since the islands could not meet all the feeding needs of the Ruhk, the creatures often flew to India, Arabia, and Africa, where they carried off all kinds of animals, even elephants.

In "The Story of Sinbad the Voyager" from *The Arabian Nights*, Sinbad relates more than one adventure with the bird called the Ruhk. In his first adventure with this creature, he was marooned on an island where he discovered a huge Ruhk egg. In order to escape, he waited until the Ruhk landed, then tied himself to one of its legs, which was as thick as a tree trunk. He described the monstrous wings as blotting out the sunlight. Unaware of its passenger, at daybreak the Ruhk flew to a steep-walled valley where she hunted for serpents to eat. Sinbad was later rescued from the valley by merchants hunting for diamonds.

On a later voyage, Sinbad was traveling with other men who stopped at an island. There they found a young Ruhk, which they killed and ate. The parents of this bird flew back from the mainland

and found the sailors feasting on their fledgling. The sailors put to sea immediately but the Ruhks took up tremendous boulders in their talons and dropped them on the ship, sinking it and killing many on board. Sinbad managed to float away on the wreckage.

The Arabs tell of another similar gigantic bird, known as an Anka. Allah supposedly created the Anka to kill and eat the wild animals of Palestine so the Israelites could move into the country. However, Allah forgot to remove the creature and the Anka made large parts of that country barren and uninhabitable.

Psychological Attributes: Positive—A person who uses his or her skills, power, and/or size to protect him or herself and family. Negative—A person who uses these abilities to bully others.

Magickal Attributes: Protection.

Hraesvelg

Scandinavian and Norse mythology mention a giant bird called Hraesvelg (or Hraesveglur). This creature symbolized storms and was said to create the wind by sitting at the end of the world (in the North),[1] overlooking Hel's realm, and beating its huge wings. The name Hraesvelg in Old Norse means "corpse-eater," but the Norse legends never mention it eating the dead. Rather, as a giant[2] it seems to represent the Land of the Dead, which to the Scandinavians was always somewhere in the North.

Psychological Attributes: Facing death and loss and being able to come to terms with the sadder aspects of life.

Magickal Attributes: Creating and/or controlling storms; a guide to the Underworld.

Imdugud

A gigantic part-bird, part-man, part-animal creature of great importance in Mesopotamian mythology was Imdugud or Zu. According to the legends, Zu stole the Tablets of Destiny from the gods themselves. Imdugud was known to the Akkadians as Anzu. It was bird-like with the body of a human, the head of a lion, and a beak like a saw. When

IMDUGUD

it flapped its great wings, it created whirlwinds and sandstorms. When still, its wings covered the entire sky like thick clouds. Its name means either "heavy rain" or "sling-stone."

A large copper panel from the temple of Ninhursag at Tell-el Obeid, near Ur, portrays a divine lion-headed eagle known as Imdugud. With this being are two stags. This panel was originally over the doorway of the temple, and is dated from about the third millennium B.C.E.

In a Sumerian myth, Imdugud or Anzu stole the Tablets of Destiny from the god Enki; the Akkadian myth says he stole the Tablets from Enlil. Both myths say that Imdugud was killed by Ninurta and the Tablets returned to the god. However, in the epic of Gilgamesh, the hero Gilgamesh saw Imdugud and one of its fledglings nesting in a sacred halub tree which Inanna had planted in Uruk.

Pictures of Zu have been found on ancient cylinder seals. One such seal shows the god Ea sitting on his throne, surrounded by water with swimming fish in it. Ea is holding Zu, who faces the Sun god Shamash as he rises from behind a mountain.

A second seal of the third millennium B.C.E. again shows the god Ea on his throne in the midst of water. Zu, the man-bird, stands before the throne, while an attendant threatens him with a spear.

Psychological Attributes: A person who tries to take shortcuts in learning spiritual and psychic disciplines.

Magickal Attributes: Controlling rain storms, whirlwinds, and sand-storms.

Raven

Another giant bird of Native American legend was Raven. This creature was thought of as both a creator/transformer and a trickster. Raven gave humans the gift of fire; he constantly creates and transforms the world and humans. Although Raven provides and cares for humans, he is always a trickster: he likes nothing better than to make life miserable and too eventful. A shape-shifter, Raven can appear in any form he chooses, including a fox, jay, or even the Moon.

Psychological Attributes: Willfully breaking loose from the natural order and universal laws. A person who thinks he or she is above the law.

Magickal Attributes: A trickster deity, much like Coyote. Very dangerous.

RAVEN

THUNDER BIRD

Thunder Bird

A huge sacred bird, primarily equated with thunder and lightning, was found in North America. Often the Thunder Bird is spoken of as more than one magickal creature, thus pointing to a species rather than an individual. It is said to live above the clouds, its gigantic flapping wings causing the thunder and its flashing eyes creating the lightning.

The Thunder Bird can never be surprised by evil (which is its perpetual enemy) because of its acute and highly magnified senses. Its attack is always signaled by the thunder of its great wings.

Psychological Attributes: One who works against any evil he or she finds.

Magickal Attributes: Knowledgeable magicians do not invoke the Thunder Bird; it comes of its own will or not at all. Enemy of all evil.

The White Eagle of Zeus

This magnificent and beautiful giant bird was the special messenger of the Greek god Zeus, and also the god's symbol among the Greek peoples. The White Eagle looked exactly like any other eagle, except for its gigantic size and glowing white feathers.

However, this magickal bird was very special. It could move easily from one plane of existence to another, even while carrying a human passenger. It was capable of communicating with both deities and humans, not by its harsh voice, but by telepathy. Whenever it appears, magicians know that an extremely important message has come from the Higher Powers.

Psychological Attributes: A person who is a sincere follower of the God/dess and who passes along spiritual messages in a form understandable to others.

Magickal Attributes: When the White Eagle appears, an important message is coming from the gods. Moving from one plane of existence to another; telepathy; communication with the deities and spiritual guides.

Other Giant Birds

The Hindus had a gigantic bird which they believed was the Sun; this great bird was considered to be either an eagle or a swan.

An eagle with human arms was a symbol of Sun worship in ancient Syria. As with the Egyptian Ba, this gigantic bird conducted souls to an afterlife.

The Japanese sky-bird, called the Pheng, was similar to the Arabian Ruhk. It could eclipse the Sun and swallow a camel.

ENDNOTES

1. This is according to the Vafprudnismal 37.
2. It is listed among the giants in the Pulur.

9

Human-Birds

The figure of a bird with human parts is not uncommon in mythology. Some of these creatures were considered benevolent toward humans, while others were dangerous and avoided.

Garuda

Garuda is one of the most fascinating and colorful of the strange creatures of Indian mythology. The Mahabharata describes him as the Bird of Life who both destroys and creates all. He is both steed and servant of the god Vishnu. Sometimes Garuda is still called upon to ease snake bite, as he is the enemy of all serpents. Garuda has the head, wings, beak, and claws of a giant eagle, but a human body and limbs. His face is white, his wings red, and his body golden. This bird-man is considered to be a kind and benevolent semi-deity.

GARUDA

His mother Vinata (also the mother of Vishnu) was the sister of Kadru, queen of the serpents. His father was Kasyapa. Before Garuda was born, or rather hatched (for his mother laid an egg), Vinata and Kadru had a disagreement over the color of the horses who were born from the churning of the Sea of Milk. Vinata was certain they were white, but Kadru swore they were black and white. The sisters made a bet about this: the loser would be a slave to the winner. Kadru wanted to win, so she sent her serpents to paint the horses with venom, thus making them appear darker than they were. Garuda's mother then became Kadra's slave. When Garuda was hatched soon afterward, he also became a slave.

Garuda was determined to free himself and his mother from his aunt's unpleasant slavery. Finally he learned that the only way to do this was to steal some of the ambrosia which belonged to the gods. After many adventures, Garuda reached the fire-barrier and the venomous snakes surrounding the ambrosia. He defeated the gods who protected it, put out the fire, and killed the snakes. Seizing the ambrosia in his claws, he flew away to his mother and freed her.

Vishnu, one of the three most important Hindu gods, was so impressed with Garuda's abilities and his devotion to his mother that the god granted him eternal life and asked him to be his companion and steed. Garuda agreed.

During the mythological battle between Rama and an army of demons (described in the Ramayana), both Rama and his brother Lakshman were fatally wounded. Garuda came from heaven like a streak of fire, touching their faces with his wings and curing them.

As king of the birds, Garuda is a tireless enemy of all snakes. The Hindus believe that he has magickal power against snake venom and pray to him if they are bitten. He can also immediately sense the presence of any evil creatures and is said to be able to track down and arrange for the punishment of bad humans.

Garuda is not only popular in India, but also in Indo-China, Siam, Cambodia, and most of southeast Asia. At Angkor, his image can be seen at the corners of the buildings, holding a snake in each hand.

There was also a similar winged man in pre-Buddhist Tibet, but little is known about him.

Psychological Attributes: Positive—A person who fights against evil wherever he or she finds it. Negative—One who has fanatical likes and dislikes.

Magickal Attributes: Learning the power of words in magick; healing. A death-like change in life. Delivering punishment to evil humans.

The Harpies

Among the many Greek fabulous beasts were the dreadful Harpies. There was never a certain total given of the number of Harpies loose in the world. The name Harpy may come from the Greek *harpyiai,* which means "snatchers" or "ravishers." These were huge, predatory birds with vulture-like bodies, the heads and faces of women, and the claws of eagles. Some sources say their wings were made of metal, which made a terrible clanging noise as they flew.

Usually the Harpies were sent on missions by the gods to punish or torment someone who had broken spiritual laws. They would swoop down upon the victim, either snatching him or her away or tormenting and tearing at the person. They also would snatch food

HARPIES

from a table, leaving behind their filth and foul stench which caused disease and famine.

Creatures of wind, storm, thunder, and lightning, the Harpies have been described as hideous beasts, but also as winged women of ethereal beauty. Mythology calls them the daughters of Thaumas and Electra. Homer names one of them as Podarge (Swiftfooted), while Hesiod mentions Aello (Stormswift) and Okypete, Ocypete, or Ocepete (Swiftwing). Other ancient writers list Celaeno (the Dark).

Their harsh, semi-human screams, the thunder of their great wings, and the foul stench of their feathers gave warning to their victims only at the last minute. It was never possible to escape the Harpy punishment sent by the gods.

Some traditions of the Mediterranean area say that one of the Harpies was drowned in the a river in the Peloponnese. Another tried to flee to the Echinade Islands where, in an attempt to turn around, she fell to the shore and was killed. These islands were called the Strophades, from the Greek word "to turn."

In Germanic heraldry one can find a creature similar in looks to the Harpy: the Frauenadler, or Jungfrauadler. This being is a woman from the navel up, but with the body, wings, tail, and legs of an eagle. The Harpy in English heraldry was borne in the arms of someone who had committed manslaughter, while this was not the case of the Frauenadler.

Psychological Attributes: One who takes a delight in deliberately harming or destroying others in some way. This can be on the spiritual, mental, or emotional levels as well as the physical.

Magickal Attributes: The dynamic but negative harmonies of cosmic energies. Punishment for those who break spiritual laws. Wind, storms, thunder and lightning.

The Sirens

Although the Greek Sirens were connected with the ocean and water, originally they were human-birds.[1] Their name is derived from a Greek root word meaning "to bind or attach." Latin adopted this word as Sirena, which went into the French as *sereine;* these sea Nymph-bird-women are sometimes called Seirenes. They had a temple at Sorrento.

SIRENS

The number of Sirens is given as two, three, four, or even eight. These sea Nymph-birds had human-sized bird bodies with the heads, arms, and breasts of women. They had beautiful, alluring voices which they used to draw sailors to their deaths on great rocks along the shore. Their favorite instrument was the lyre or double flute. The Sirens sang love songs while sitting on the sea rocks. Any man who heard their singing was instantly enchanted, jumped from the ship, and drowned. However, the Sirens, like the Minotaur, had a liking for human flesh.

Many tales of the origin of the Sirens are contradictory. They were at one time water Nymphs, children of the river god Achelous and the Nymph Calliope. Changed from their Nymph form by Ceres, they also seem to be related in some manner to Persephone, Queen of the Underworld.

The names commonly given for them were Aglaophonos or Aglaophone (of the brilliant voice), Thelxepeia (of the words which enchant), Peisinoe (the persuasive), and Molpe (song). Other writers add the names of Parthenope, Ligeia, and Leukosia.

Because of their vanity about their voices and pride in their musical talent, myth says that the Sirens one day challenged the Muses to a musical contest. The Muses won and punished the Sirens by pulling out their wing feathers. Ashamed of their appearance, these bird-women left the springs and dales to hide among the jagged rocks along the coast of southern Italy. They took up residence at Cape Pelorus, Capri, the isle of Anthemusa, and the Siren Isles.

When Ulysses had to sail past the island where the Sirens lived, he stuffed wax in the ears of his men, then had them tie him to the mast. In this way, the Greek hero could hear the Sirens' song but not be able to jump from the ship in an effort to join them.

The Greeks recorded the adventures of only one other hero who managed to escape the enchantment of the Sirens: Jason of the Argo. With Jason and the Argonauts was the highly skilled harp player Orpheus. When the Argo reached the Sirens' isle, Orpheus began to play his harp and sing. All but one of the Argonauts was able to resist the lure of these sea Nymphs. Buto leaped overboard, but was rescued by Aphrodite.

According to an ancient prophecy, the Sirens would become great stones when they failed to lure seamen to their deaths. When they failed to attract the sailors of the Argo, the Sirens leaped into the ocean where they turned into dangerous sunken rocks. Tradition says that the body of one of them, Parthenope, was cast up on the shore at the place where the city of Naples was later built.

Much of the material on Sirens is found in the writings of Aristotle, Pliny, Ovid, and Hyginus, and in the *Physiologus* (about the second century C.E.) and the medieval bestiaries.

Sirens seemed not to be only Greek creatures. On one of Columbus' voyages, he recorded that he and his men had seen Sirens.

Psychological Attributes: The lure of spending too much time delving into psychic or spiritual matters, which will lead to imbalance in one's personal life.

Magickal Attributes: Singing; love spells.

Tengu

The Tengu [tin-goo] of Japan are strange half-bird, half-human creatures. They have the body of a man and the face of a bird and carry a fan made of feathers. Their main purpose in life appears to be to cause trouble, particularly by teaching humans how to use weapons of war. They are woodland creatures with a character partly like the Nature spirit Pan and partly like a poltergeist. On occasion they will possess a human, causing their victim to show great skill in

TENGU

dancing and weapons. When the Tengu spirit is driven out, the human remembers nothing. These beings are said to be able to shape-shift into any animal form and have great magickal powers.

Creatures of the old Shinto religion, the Tengu were the fierce enemies of Buddhism during the Middle Ages. They loved to tempt, fool, or carry off priests, or set fire to the temples. This antagonism may have come about because the Tengu wanted their worship restored, something forbidden by the Buddhists. The Buddhist hell even had a place called the "Tengu road," an area said to be reserved for hypocritical priests who had fallen into sin and forsaken their vows.

Some Japanese who live in the more remote regions still believe in the Tengu. Today, the creatures are said to be sharp-eyed bird-like spirits who haunt isolated areas and, if not given offerings, play pranks on travelers or steal lost children.

An ancient Japanese hanging scroll portrays a creature similar to the Tengu. This being has a woman's head, arms, breasts, and torso; its back legs are bird's feet, and it has two wings and a long feathery tail.

Psychological Attributes: Positive—One who is attracted to the Old Religions, rejecting the accepted modern ones. Negative—A follower of a specific religion who is constantly shoving his or her personal beliefs in the faces of non-believers.

Magickal Attributes: Very dangerous, as they like to possess humans and through them cause violent trouble, although the Tengu have great magickal power. Dance, weapons, war.

Other Human-Birds

In Irish Celtic myth a bird-like being appeared to Mess Buachalla and made love to her. The offspring of this union was a son called Conaire Mess Buachalla.

Many of the surviving bas-reliefs in Babylon, Assyria, and Mesopotamia show a distinct type of human-bird creature. These have been named "genies" by archaeologists. They were mostly considered to be benevolent creatures of wisdom and protection from disease, although there were a few, like the demon Pazuzu, who were evil. They also had the power to drive away evil spirits and demons.

Many of these beings were pictured taking part in rituals. Not all of them were male; one female figure holding a chaplet of beads is shown. The Akkadian term *aladlammu* appears to have been the name generally given to these genii, as well as to bulls and lions with human heads.

Pazuzu was an Assyrian and Babylonian winged demon genie of the first millennium B.C.E. Pictures of this evil being show a scaly but human-like body with bulging eyes, a dog-like face, wings, bird talons, and a snake-headed penis. Although Pazuzu was basically evil, he was a balance against such creatures as Lamastu and the pestilential winds.

On a bronze amulet of the ninth to seventh centuries B.C.E, the demon Pazuzu is shown as a four-winged creature with three-toed bird's feet, a human-like body, and a terrible face.

On one of the gates of the palace of Sargon II at Khorsabad, just beyond statues of the great winged bulls, is a sculpture of a winged genie. The head is that of an eagle; the human body is clothed in a long fringed robe and a horned headdress. In its hands it holds a lustral vase and pine cone sprinkler, with which it spiritually purifies all those who enter the palace. This carving dates from the eighth century B.C.E. On a marble Assyrian bas-relief from about 885 B.C.E. is another representation of the winged genie. This one also holds the water vase and pine cone sprinkler. On his feet are sandals, and a dagger is thrust in a belt around his waist.

Another Assyrian stone bas-relief, from about 883-859 B.C.E., portrays the emperor Ashur-nazir-pal II with an eagle-headed winged genie. This genie is using the sprinkler and vase to purify the king.

A four-winged genie is shown on the jamb of the gateway at Pasargadae; the inscription in three languages states that Cyrus the Achaemenid built it. Similar winged genii stand at the gatehouse of Xerxes I. They have human forms with great double wings.

Psychological Attributes: Being alert and aware of the hidden intentions of malicious people and defending yourself and others from them.

Magickal Attributes: Winged genie—Spiritually purifies. Pazuzu—Basically evil and very dangerous; not recommended.

BA BIRDS

The Egyptian Ba

Ancient Egyptian hieroglyphs and paintings show a human-headed bird called the Ba. This figure was said to represent one of the seven souls belonging to each person. In later Greek and Roman art, this same human-bird figure can be seen and has the same meaning.

In a number of mythologies around the world, certain birds were considered to be souls of the dead. Sometimes these birds have human heads, sometimes not.

ENDNOTES

1. Later, the Sirens were said to have fish-tails for the lower half of their bodies. However, they were bird-humans originally.

10

Griffins

The Griffin's name is sometimes spelled Gryphon or Griffon. It was a half-bird, half-mammal creature. An enormous beast, it had the wings, foreparts, front legs, and head of an eagle, with the rear-parts, hind paws, tail, and ears of a lion. Some writers believed its tail was long and serpentine. Said to be the offspring of an eagle and a lion, the Griffin was thought to be eight times larger than a lion and stronger than a hundred eagles. Its coloring varied from tawny to golden, cream flecked with scarlet, or pure white. The feathers on the head and wings could be blue or green, while the breast feathers were often scarlet. The eagle-like beak and legs were golden, the talons black. The Griffin's young were hatched from eggs, and were very gentle when little.

In European and Mediterranean art and sculpture, it was shown lying down or sitting on its haunches. Part of an old Armenian carpet design shows a Griffin with a human head and a dragon-like tail.

The fierce, intelligent Griffin was known throughout the Near and Middle East, including Greece. Legend says it lived in India, Turkey, Armenia, Syria, and Iraq, all semi-arid regions where large deposits of precious gems were once known to exist. In Assyria and the East, the Griffin was called the "cloud-cleaving eagle" and "the king of beasts." In India and Scythia, it was given a name meaning "Bird of Gold," because the people of these cultures said it guarded gold mines.

The Mesopotamian Griffin had a crested head, while the head of the Greek creature was pictured with a mane of tight spiral curls. The Babylonians and Persians had similar beasts with wings, eagle-heads, goat-beards, and lion-bodies.

The keen-eared Griffin was considered to be the guardian of hidden treasure,[1] particularly the gold mines of India and Scythia. It was said to build its gold-lined nest in the mountains of those regions. Associated with the Sun and the Golden Apples of Hera, the Griffin was also said to guard the "jewels" of the stars.[2] Each claw was as large as an antelope horn; these were sometimes made into drinking cups because, like the horn of the Unicorn, they changed color when poison was present. Medieval scholars wrote that the Griffin was especially hostile toward horses. A Griffin was said to be able to carry off a full-sized horse.

An old Italian story tells of a blind king whose eyesight was restored by a Griffin feather dipped in oil. To get this feather, the king's youngest son went on a perilous journey to the northern mountains, where he found a Griffin's nest and retrieved a feather. He returned with this feather and cured his father.

The Griffin, like similar birds, was majestic, aloof, but kind in early legendary tales. As encounters with Griffins spread to the West, however, this creature came to be feared, probably because humans began to hunt them, as they did Dragons.

There is a Norse tale about Hagen, a king's son, who was carried off by a Griffin to a high mountain as a meal for its young. He survived by escaping and hiding in a cave. When a suit of armor washed up on the beach near his cave, Hagen wore it to protect himself while killing all the Griffins.

When European merchants of the twelfth century went on perilous voyages to China and other distant countries, they carried with

GRIFFIN

them the complete skins of animals, which could be hermetically sealed to hide them. Then, if the ship sank or they ran out of supplies, they could dress in these skins. Griffins, seeing what they believed to be animals, would catch them in their claws and carry them to their mountain nesting places. The disguised men then had only to unfasten the skins and kill the Griffins.

In the Middle Ages, Sir John Mandeville wrote of seeing a Griffin in Bacharia. He described the creature as stronger than a hundred lions or eagles.

In ancient Greek and Roman mythologies, the chariots of Jupiter, Apollo, and Nemesis were said to be drawn by Griffins. Legend says, however, that the Griffins of Nemesis (goddess of retribution) were different from other Griffins, in that their bodies and feathers were completely black. These creatures were especially sacred to Nemesis as instruments of vengeance.

Some historians say that Griffins were part of the monstrous band which accompanied the Mesopotamian goddess Tiamat. Even the ancient Egyptian falcon-headed lion reminds one of the Griffin.

As the guardian of the pathway to spiritual enlightenment, the Griffin was usually shown next to a Tree of Life or a similar symbol. It symbolized the seasons and guarded the Sun, the sacred Golden Apples, and treasures. It is one of the oldest and most popular symbols in heraldry.

Tyler, in the third edition of *Early History of Mankind,* describes a Griffin's claw that once belonged to Corpus Christi College, Cambridge. This claw was never identified as belonging to any commonly known creature. In *Heraldry in History, Poetry & Romance* by E. J. Millington it is mentioned that the treasury at Bayeux had three Griffin claws which were exhibited on the altar on feast days. Henry the Lion was said to have brought back a Griffin's claw from Palestine; it is now said to be in Brunswick Cathedral.

Psychological Attributes: Positive—Seeing a Griffin is a sign of powerful new beginnings, of learning how to use the psychic in a useful manner. Negative—Subconscious punishment for love of riches, greed, or for desiring riches. This often occurs because of negative religious teaching.

Magickal Attributes: Understanding the relationship between psychic energy and cosmic forces. Spiritual wisdom and enlightenment. Bringing the dark side of ourselves into submission. As a powerful guardian entity, vigilance and vengeance. A coming time of great magick.

Griffin-Demons

In a wonderful wall painting done with glazed bricks in Darius' palace at Susa is a scene showing Lion-Griffins, creatures later used by the Babylonians. The Lion-Griffin had the head and body of a lion, the hind feet and wings of an eagle, and a centrally joined horn with two branches on its head. The Griffin-Demon, typical on Middle Assyrian seals, had a human body with a bird's head and wings.

On magick wands of the New Kingdom in ancient Egypt one can see the form of the Griffin-Demon, with a winged lion's body and the head of a falcon. It is often shown pulling a chariot and leading the magician to victory over evil creatures. The Griffin-Demon of Egypt was used in positive magick.

Psychological Attributes: One who has learned the powerful art of creating through the use of magick, and uses this power for good.

Magickal Attributes: The making of magick wands.

Hippogriff

The Hippogriff or Hippogriffin was a combination of the horse and Griffin. Mythology says its mother was a mare and the father a Griffin. The Hippogriff was said to live in the far north on rocky crags in mountainous areas. It had the body of a horse and the front part of a Griffin with beak, claws, and wings.

It was found primarily in stories from the Middle Ages about Charlemagne and his knights. The epic poem *Orlando Furioso,* by Ariosto, gives great detail about the Hippogriff; the hero is given the Hippogriff as an indefeatable mount. It was also the unpredictable mount of the Wizard Atlantis.

Since the Hippogriff is an astral creature who can take you to the doorway of the path of spiritual enlightenment, you must be certain that you are properly prepared to make the journey and learn this knowledge. The Hippogriff will take you, if you are prepared or not. However, upon arrival, if you have only talked yourself into

HIPPOGRIFF

believing you are prepared or have the wrong motives for taking the journey, the Hippogriff will deliver you into some very disturbing astral experiences. This will cure you of any false sense of your great spiritual training and preparedness.

Psychological Attributes: Positive—One who has learned the delicate balance of the physical, mental, emotional, and spiritual necessary for magick. Negative—One who has not learned to work well under the supervision or direction of authority.

Magickal Attributes: A powerful mount to ride between Worlds during meditations.

Senmurv

Early Persian myths tell of the Senmurv or Sinamru, an immortal bird-mammal creature. The name Senmurv possibly means "dog-bird," meaning a creature of two natures and having access to two worlds. It had wings which darkened the sky when it flew, but it also

SENMURV

had teeth. The females suckled their young as do mammals. Sometimes it was shown in art as having a dog-like head and paws, but the wings and tail of a bird.

In the Sasanian art of the Middle East, the Senmurv is often seen as a kind of dragon-peacock. Except for its wide feathered tail, it looks like a Griffin on a silver ewer from that period.

Legends of the Senmurv say that in the beginning it was a friend and helper of humans. It lived in a tree guarded by 99,999 spirits. The seeds of this tree could cure all evil; every time the Senmurv landed in the tree, it shook loose thousands of these seeds, which scattered over the Earth and cured human illnesses. This creature was a deadly enemy of all snakes. The Senmurv may be a form of the Simurgh.

Psychological Attributes: One who has developed healing abilities.

Magickal Attributes: Use to access other Worlds during meditations and magickal workings; deadly enemy of all snakes and evil.

Simurgh

Later Persian legends tell of the Simurgh, another giant bird which nested on the highest peaks of the Alburz Mountains in northern Persia. This magickal, mythical beast, written about in the Shah-Nameh, had lion claws, peacock plumes, a snake tail, and a Griffin head. The Simurgh was half-bird, half-mammal, and suckled its young. One legend says it lived for 1700 years. Like the Indian Garuda, the Simurgh hated snakes.

In the eleventh century, the Persian poet Firdausi recorded the legends of the Simurgh, Rustam the giant, and the child Zal. Rustam was a great legendary hero of the Persian culture. His birth came about through the incantations of a wizard. This wizard was approached by the Simurgh and was loaned some of the bird's magickal feathers to produce this unusual child. This Simurgh was pictured as red with long tail-feathers.

Rustam was not considered to be an ordinary man. He was described as being as tall as eight men, with the strength and courage of a lion. Of course, this hero would ride no ordinary horse. He searched throughout the country until he caught one that had the strength of an elephant and the speed of a racing camel. In part

SIMURGH

of his adventures, Rustam defeated, with the help of the Simurgh, an ambitious and evil prince called Isfandiyar.

A benevolent creature, the Simurgh lived in a land where the sacred *haoma* plant also grew. This plant was sometimes called the Tree of Life. The seeds of the *haoma* were said to cure all diseases and evil. The Simurgh gathered these and flew over the world, scattering the seeds. This fabulous beast had prophetic and magickal powers, great wisdom, and healing qualities in its feathers.

The Caucasus area and Russia also had stories of creatures with similar names: Simargl, Simyr, Sinam. Like the Simurgh, these creatures could help humans communicate between one world and another.

In Armenia, this creature was called the Sinam. A story tells of a young prince who had to make a dangerous journey to the Underworld as part of a trial imposed upon him. To leave he had to jump onto a black goat which would throw him onto a lighter-colored goat; this process would be repeated until he reached the outer world again. He was careless, however, and forgot the instructions for returning. He jumped onto a white goat first and found himself trapped in the Underworld. He had many perilous and frightening adventures before a Sinam carried him back to this world.

In Iranian tradition, the Simurgh was shown as a composite creature made of features from the peacock, lion, Griffin, and dog. It was considered a bird of good omen. However, in the Shah-Nameh, the Simurgh is called a noble "vulture." The legend given there says that this creature rescued Zal, the baby son of Sam, and raised him on Mount Elburz. Sam was the governor of Hindustan. Part of this legend is shown on a golden Persian dish of the sixth to seventh centuries C.E.

Psychological Attributes: See Senmurv.

Magickal Attributes: Curing all diseases and banishing evil; prophetic and magickal powers; wisdom, healing; communication between one plane of existence and another.

Endnotes

1. Arnold Whittick. *Symbols: Signs & Their Meaning & Uses in Design.*
2. Ibid.

11

Mystical Bulls and Bull-Men

Half-human, half-bull figures are frequently seen in ancient sculptures and drawings. The best known of these is the Minotaur. Some of these bull-forms were mostly human, while others had fewer human features. These images symbolize the desire for human control over animal emotions and instincts.

Minotaur

The Cretan Minotaur is a form of the man-bull. Legend says this creature was born from the union of the Cretan queen Parsiphae and the Minoan sacred bull. The name comes from *tauros*, the sacred bull, and Minos, "one dedicated to the Moon."[1]

Long ago in Crete, a magnificent white bull was set aside as a sacrifice to the sea god Poseidon. King Minos (Moon-King), however, desired to keep the bull for himself and substituted another bull in its place at the sacrifice. Poseidon was furious at this trickery and caused the king's wife Parsiphae to develop a fierce lust for the white bull. To consummate her lust, the queen ordered the artisan Daedalus to build a female cow. Parsiphae hid herself inside the artificial cow and mated with the white bull.

King Minos was not the least suspicious when Parsiphae became pregnant, but when the child was born it had the head of a bull. Minos knew immediately that he had been punished by Poseidon. He dared not kill the strange creature for fear of bringing further divine retribution upon himself.

The Minotaur proved to be a violent creature; as it grew, it developed a taste for human flesh. Eventually, Minos had to build the famous underground labyrinthine prison where he confined the Minotaur. He instituted the annual famous Bull-Dances, levying a tribute of young people from each section of his empire. Those dancers who could outwit the Minotaur were promoted to bull-leapers and performed their acrobatic dances with a real bull before crowds of spectators. Those who did not outwit the Minotaur died in his labyrinthine prison at his hands. Finally, the Minotaur was slain by the Greek hero Perseus.

The sacred Cretan bull-leapers had special dances and acrobatics they did with a real sacred bull at specific festivals before crowds of Cretans. Their daring movements later became some of the classic moves of the present-day bullfighter. This dance with the sacred bull was in honor of Poseidon, the Cretan king Minos, and the legendary Minotaur. To honor the Minotaur, these bull-leapers sometimes wore bull-head masks; not, however, during their sacred dances.[2]

The Minotaur signifies the animal passions of humans which can rage out of control if not balanced by spiritual understanding.

Psychological Attributes: Predominance of the animal-aspects in humans.

Magickal Attributes: Supernatural strength; protection. Protection without revenge, but through spiritual power.

MINOTAUR

Other Human-Headed Bulls

Figures of men with the heads of bulls first appeared in the third millennium B.C.E. in the Middle Eastern empires. Cylinder seals of this era clearly show a human male with a horned bull's head. Sometimes these Bull-Men were shown in combat with human male heroes. By the Old Babylonian and Kassite Periods, this Bull-Man appeared not only in combat, but as an attendant to the Sun god Shamash. By Neo-Assyrian times, the Bull-Man was shown holding or supporting the winged disk, a symbol of Shamash. The Sumerian word *gud-alim* gave the name *kusarikku* to the bull-headed man as well as to the human-headed bull.

In India, the god Yama sometimes wore a bull's head. As Lord of Death, Yama was ruler of the Underworld,[3] judge of the dead, and god of truth and righteousness. He was the brother-husband of his twin sister Yami. The Hindus say that Yama judges the *dharma* (earthly duty) of humans. He was also called Pitripati (father of

YAMA

fathers), Sraddaheva (god of funerals), Samana (the leveller), and Dandadhara (the beater or punisher). He was accompanied by brindled watchdogs with four eyes. The Hindus say Yama currently resides in Yamapura.[4]

Dionysus, in his earlier Cretan form of Zagreus, was a bull-headed, human-figured god. He was called the "Goodly Bull," and was considered to be a son of Zeus. Dionysus, in this form, may well be another version of the Minotaur. Mythology tells us that Zagreus was considered to be a bull-headed man on Earth, worshipped in the form of the sacred bull, but a serpent in his regenerating Underworld form.[5]

Ancient Armenian mythology mentions a kingdom called Urartu, which lay around Lake Van (now in Turkey). One impressive remnant of this culture is a cast-bronze figurine of a winged bull with a human head and torso, from about 750 B.C.E.

Psychological Attributes: Positive—Understanding the Underworld and the dead, but not getting caught up in fatalistic thoughts. Negative—Unreasonable fear of death and the dead.

Magickal Attributes: Human-headed bulls—See Minotaur. Yama—Truth, earthly duty, judgment, destiny, death, and punishment.

Winged Bull

The massive figure of the winged bull can still be seen in Assyrian and Sumero-Semitic sculptures. The Assyrians called this being the Shedu or Shedim.[6] They carved his image in stone as guardian of the gates and doors of their temples and palaces. The winged bull had a man's head with a crown and the body of a bull with wings.

An eighth-century B.C.E. sculpture from the palace of Sargon II at Khorsabad is of such a winged bull. A guardian of the palace, it wears a horned headdress and is sculpted with five legs. Although an awe-inspiring figure, the Shedu were said to be benevolent beings and were usually shown in pairs.

The Shedu are extremely powerful. These magickal creatures have their own language, as do many others listed in this book. However, they are very intelligent and can understand any language used by humans. Although the Shedu have this special ability, they prefer to communicate with humans by telepathy, or direct mind contact. They are adept at all psychic powers, using these abilities only for good. Although these beasts originated

SHEDU

in the Middle East, they like to travel all over the world, working against evil, helping those humans who are in desperate need and those magicians who ask their aid in positive spellwork.

Assyrian Shedu, or winged bulls, symbolize humans with their spiritual wings, human heads, and beast bodies. The five legs portrayed on statues of the Shedu represent the five Elements of Earth, Air, Fire, Water, and Spirit.

The Shedu are excellent guides in the search for ancient occult knowledge, usually discovered on astral journeys. They will work only with those humans who have high ideals and goals. Any rudeness, commands, or breach of morals will cause them to sever any arrangement immediately without further contact.

Psychological Attributes: A magician who has learned the importance of the five Elements and how to use them in balance. A non-magickal person who balances all aspects and responsibilities in his or her life.

Magickal Attributes: Extremely powerful; will work with positive spellworking only. Magick, languages, telepathy, all psychic powers, working against evil.

ENDNOTES

1. Barbara Walker. *The Woman's Dictionary of Symbols & Sacred Objects.*
2. Ibid.
3. Joseph Campbell. *Mythic Image.*
4. Anne S. Baumgartner. *A Comprehensive Dictionary of the Gods.*
5. Francis Legge. *Forerunners & Rivals of Christianity.*
6. The term *shedim* was used by the Hebrews.

12

Fabulous Lions

Mythologies present lion-men, winged lions, horned lions, lion-dogs, and many related beings. However, the history of some of these creatures has been lost.

In the temples of India, for example, there are stone carvings of horned lions, but myth and history are silent about them before Buddhists adopted their already existing forms. A Persian miniature shows a lion with stag's horns and a flaming tail, while a stone carving from an Indian temple portrays a lion with three horns. This lion has one horn in the center of its head and one on each side of this horn; it has pointed ears and a large ruff or mane.

The lion, in any of its many forms, was associated with the Sun, regalness, and fearlessness. Many place-names, ancient and modern, have some connection with the lion, reflecting the universal respect for this creature. Since the ancient people looked beyond the ordinary animal in most things, they must have been referring to the supernatural form of the lion, rather than the mundane one. In England, Caerleon (the Lion's Place) was the city of Merlin the magician. An ancient name for Cornwall was Lyonesse (Country of the She-lion). The name Singapore means "city of the lion." Simhasana (the Lion Throne) is still held sacred in Buddhism.

Medical texts from medieval times give much credit to images of lions and their uses in healing magick.[1]

Akeru

The Akeru was a strange two-headed creature from ancient Egyptian myths.[2] Its joined, reclining body had two lions' heads facing opposite directions, and two sets of front legs. The back parts of each lion merged into each other. On their heads was the Sun disk. Their names were sometimes given as Xerefu and Akeru, or Sef and Tuau. As the Lions of Yesterday and Today, they guarded the gates of sunrise and sunset, and were considered to be a symbol of time.[3] Their symbolism was similar to the Greek designation of Alpha and Omega.

Psychological Attributes: Positive—One who can look at the past without too many regrets, yet look toward the future with hope. Negative—One who seldom makes a decision if he or she can avoid it.

Magickal Attributes: Looking backward through time to learn from mistakes made in past lives.

The Chimera

The Chimera, sometimes spelled Chimaera, lived in Lydia, in Asia Minor. Myth says that this female creature was born to Typhon and Echidna. She was said to be a fire-breathing monster, with the front part of a lion and the tail of a Dragon. She also had three heads: those of a goat, lion, and Dragon. In medieval art, the Chimera was often portrayed with the goat's head growing out of the middle of her back.

One classical myth says the Chimera was a divine Nymph. However, the best-known story says she was a fire-breathing monster

CHIMERA

who constantly wreaked havoc throughout the Lydian district and neighboring areas until Bellerophon, with the help of Pegasus, killed her. Although there was believed to be only one Chimera, many statues of this creature show her with the swollen teats of a nursing lioness.

Although the Chimera is usually associated with the Mediterranean and Near Eastern cultures, a bronze statue from the Han Dynasty clearly portrays a Chimera with two horns, a wrinkled nose, a feathery tail, and curled designs all over its body.

The word Chimera comes from the Greek *chimaira,* or "she-goat," which is related to the Greek word *cheimon,* "winter." Today it means an illusion or fabrication of the mind.

Psychological Attributes: A person who seldom, if ever, allows his or her true self to be seen by others; the person hides behind false masks of personality. One who fabricates a "reality" and refuses to face facts.

Magickal Attributes: Call upon the Chimera when it is necessary to hide your fear or anxiety from others. The Chimera can be very dangerous, though, and should be sought only as a last resort.

Chinese Lion-Dogs

The Fu-Dogs (sometimes called Lion-Dogs or Fo-Dogs) were thought of as guardians, and statues of them were placed outside temple doors. The little flat faces on these statues remind one of Oriental short-faced dogs, such as the Pekingese, Tibetan spaniel, lhasa apso, and pug.

The Chinese had small physical guard dogs to hunt and kill mice, roaches, and other small vermin. These little animals, also known as Demon Catchers, were considered capable of hunting down and driving away troublesome evil spirits in this world; their barking was said to drive the evil from any house. The ancient Chinese believed that all evils are very small when they first enter this world. Therefore, little but vigilant physical animals were capable of killing or driving these evils away.

Centuries before the Forbidden City was built at Peking, at a time when the emperor lived in another city, the bravest and most intelligent of the Chinese war dogs were bred not only for loyalty, courage, and wisdom, but for smallness of size. It seems that the Chinese were duplicating in the physical an animal they knew to exist in

CHINESE LION-DOG

the spiritual. No one knows exactly how far back in history these little dogs were bred, but Chinese art of the fourteenth century shows them. By the Ch'ing or Manchu Dynasty, the Pekingese dogs were kept only by royalty for this purpose. It was considered a crime for anyone other than the royal family to own such dogs. The Empress Dowager Tzu Hsi was extremely fond of the Pekingese breed; her favorite Peke was named Shadza ("Fool").

At the end of the Second Opium War in 1860, British troops looted the imperial palaces at Peking. Four Pekingese were taken to England; one was presented to Queen Victoria. From this time through the early nineteenth century, a few other Pekingese were obtained by bribes to the palace eunuchs. Finally, in 1906, the breed was given AKC registry, with the first show held in January of 1911.

By 1924 the last Manchu emperor left the Forbidden City, bringing the imperial system in China to an end. The eunuchs then killed all the remaining Pekingese to keep them out of what they called "unworthy hands."

The Buddhist Lion-Dog is a fierce but benevolent creature who acts as a guardian and defender of Buddhist law. The Chinese Lion-Dogs are portrayed with a ball under one foot, symbolizing the balance of opposites: the defined and the undefined.

The Oriental stone lions, whether Lion-Dogs or other creatures, were said to come alive at night and make their protective rounds of the places they guarded.

Carved examples of these Lion-Dogs can still be seen in exhibits of ancient Chinese artifacts. On one Chinese jade seal is a Fo-Dog who looks exactly like a Peke. A black soapstone statue from the twentieth century shows a Fo-Dog who looks like a cross between a small lion and a Peke.

The presence and power of the Lion-Dog or Fu-Dog can be enticed into an appropriate statue of this creature through magick or by sincerely requesting the presence of the Lion-Dog. Such a statue will then become a house guardian.

Psychological Attributes: A person who can be fierce but benevolent; one having a balance of opposites within their personality.

Magickal Attributes: Guardians against evil; Demon Catchers who will drive evil out of any house.

THE MAN-LION OF VISHNU

The Man-Lion

Indian carvings and sculptures of the Man-Lion portray the god Vishnu in one of his aspects. Prahlada was a good demon who worshipped Vishnu. His father tormented him for this, saying Vishnu had no real power. The son declared that Vishnu was everywhere and saw and heard everything; the father sarcastically asked if the god was in the central pillar of his throne room. Suddenly, Vishnu leaped out of the pillar in the form of a Man-Lion. Angry at the way the demon father treated his son and at the disbelief the demon expressed, Vishnu as the Man-Lion disemboweled the demon king.

The Hindu god Vishnu, in his aspect as the Man-Lion, represents the half-fierce, half-tame nature within all creatures, even humans.

Psychological Attributes: Positive—A person who understands, controls, and uses anger in the proper manner. Negative—One who revels in his or her temper.

Magickal Attributes: Defense, particularly in a case of religious persecution and harassment.

Manticore

The Manticore was said to live in the Asian forests, particularly those of India, Malaysia, and Indonesia. The *Cambridge Bestiary* lists the Manticore as being of Indian origin. This creature was considered more dangerous than any other of the jungle dwellers. Its den or lair was often in a cave or underground hole.

The Manticore had the body of a lion and a head resembling that of a human, except for its three rows of sharp teeth. Some members of this species also had small bat-brown wings, although nothing is ever said about a Manticore flying. Its tail, however, was long and scaled like a snake. The tip of the tail had poison darts which could be thrown; natives believed these darts were made poisonous with the juice of the upas tree.

The Manticore would either stalk its victim or use its hypnotic gaze, getting close enough to hit the animal or human with the poisoned darts. Then it would tear the victim to pieces.

The earliest example of the Manticore (or Mantyger) in English heraldry is the badge of Sir William Hastings of Kirby and Burton Hastings in Warwickshire.

MANTICORE

Psychological Attributes: One who likes to "kill" for the sake and thrill of killing; this can mean "killing" a reputation or destroying someone's confidence or dreams, as well as a physical murder.

Magickal Attributes: Dangerous; not recommended.

The Sea-Lion

The fabulous creature known as the Sea-Lion is not the aquatic creature with which we are familiar. This magickal beast has the foreparts and maned head of a lion, and the silvery rear-parts of a great fish. Its strong jaws and clawed and webbed forelimbs make it very dangerous. They usually live in packs along rocky seacoasts, hunting schools of fish or shipwrecked sailors. The bellowing roars of this Sea-Lion can be heard even underwater. The Sea-Lion, like the Sea-Pegasus, is associated with the Water-Folk of the seas.

The Sea-Lion symbolizes the protective instincts of humans for children, especially their own. When human emotions are aroused

SEA-LION

because of a threat to a child, a person can become lion-like, bellowing with rage and bravely defending the victim.

Psychological Attributes: Positive—A person who has learned to bellow "foul!" when someone begins playing mind or emotional games. Negative—One who is so ultra-sensitive emotionally (and enjoys this) that he or she is upset at the slightest emotional ripple and even imagines slights when there are none.

Magickal Attributes: Defense against people who play games with your emotions and mind.

Winged Lions and Lion-Men

The winged lion is a common creature portrayed in paintings, art, and sculpture throughout the Middle East. A fifth-century Persian gold rhyton (drinking vessel) was made to look like the front part of a winged lion, with the forepart of the lion as the base of the conical rhyton. The head and face resemble an ordinary lion, but the body is covered with what looks like scales or feathers. An example of a winged lion in English heraldry is in the seal of John Hoo of Norfolk from the latter part of the thirteenth century.

Lion-headed men are found on ancient sculptures and bas-reliefs of the Middle East. Ruins have many winged genii (as they are called) with human heads, lion bodies, and wings. Other forms of this being are human from the waist up, but with two lion's legs on lion's hind-quarters with a curled-over lion's tail. The Lion-Man was a protective creature; his Akkadian name was *uridimmu,* "mad lion."

LION-DEMON

Yet another form of the Lion-Demon was a human-bodied figure with the head of a lion, upright donkey ears, a curled-up lion's
tail, and bird feet. Usually this being was shown wearing a short kilt
and holding a mace in one hand and a dagger in the other; he was
a good genie who worked against evil demons and diseases. A type
of lion-centaur also appears in Assyrian art. This creature had a
lion's body with four legs, and the upper body, head, and arms of a
human male. He was called *urmahlullu* (lion-man). His form was
placed outside ablution rooms so he could protect against the Lion-
Demon Mikil-res-lemutti (evil attendant). One can only speculate as
to what this "evil attendant" did; perhaps he represented tainted
water or thieves who attacked the bathers.

A Babylonian terracotta sculpture of about the seventh or
eighth century B.C.E. shows such a lion-headed being with a man's
body. This may have represented one of the evil genii who were said
to have been born in the Mountain of the West and who lived in
holes in the ground or among old ruins. They spread discord and
disease among humans and tried to decimate their flocks.

Another bas-relief, from 1050–850 B.C.E., portrays a different
lion-being. This one has a human head on the body of a lion, but it
also has wings. It is wearing a tall headdress, similar to the white
crown of Upper Egypt. This lion-man is a protective being, not like
the evil genii.

Psychological Attributes: Positive—A person who is protective of
close friends and family. Negative—One who likes to bring discord
and grief to others.

Magickal Attributes: Be certain that you call upon only the positive
lion-men and lion-genii. A symbol of many Sun deities, the lion symbolizes spiritual Fire. Courage in the face of continual struggle; dignity; victory; the search for spiritual enlightenment. Protection
against evil spirits and diseases.

ENDNOTES

1. Paul E. Desautels. *The Gem Kingdom.*
2. E. A. Wallis Budge. *Gods of the Egyptians.*
3. Ibid.

13

Magickal Serpents

Serpents of all kinds, in a great many cultures, were considered to be symbols of Goddess and/or Kundalini power. They were also thought to be immortal because they shed their skins, thus seeming to renew their life forever. To the Greeks, this cast-off skin was called *geras*, "old age." The Serpent-Folk can be either positive or negative, so one must take great care in working with them.

Most people have a built-in aversion to snakes, not only because of their potential danger, but because of the propaganda from the Christians and their story of the garden of Eden.

The serpent symbolizes the Kundalini power rising through the seven chakras. This process occurs naturally as a person grows spiritually. However, the Kundalini energy can turn deadly (physically, mentally, and spiritually) if it is forced upward before a person is properly spiritually prepared.

ACHELOUS

Achelous

This Greek demi-god was one of the sons of Oceanus and Tethys and the most celebrated river god. Hesiod said that there were 3,000 river-sons of this couple; they were all portrayed as vigorous men with long beards and a pair of horns on their brows.

Achelous is shown in Greek art as having a human head with horns and a human upper body and arms, but the lower body of a serpent. He presided over the largest watercourse in Greece.

Legend says that Achelous fell in love with a beautiful human maiden named Deianeira. Before she succumbed to his desires, though, the hero Heracles decided he too wanted the girl. There was a terrible battle between Achelous and Heracles. During the struggle, Achelous shape-shifted first into a serpent, then into a wild bull. Eventually Heracles tore off one of the river god's horns and defeated him. The river Nymphs took this discarded horn and turned it into the Horn of Plenty.

The river god was testy about being shown honor during sacrifices. When the daughters of the soothsayer Echinus failed in this duty, they were changed into the Echinades Islands.

Achelous was invoked throughout Greece and even in Sicily when taking oaths.

Psychological Attributes: Positive—A person who has learned to truly love another. Negative—One who will not let go without a fuss when a friendship or relationship has ended.

Magickal Attributes: Oaths, contracts, promises.

Feathered Serpent

The Feathered Serpent was known to the Aztecs and other cultures of Central America. The Mayans called him Kulkulcan, while the Aztecs named him Quetzalcoatl. This feathered creature (sometimes called plumed) was a combination of bird and snake, unlike the bat-winged serpents of the Middle East and Egypt. This bird-snake had feathers on its head, on its tail, and sometimes on its body. The Feathered Serpent appears to have been both a magickal creature and an aspect or symbol of the god Quetzalcoatl or Kulkulcan.

This serpent deity was worshipped by several Middle American cultures. Legend says he was born to Itztli (Obsidian), but the name

QUETZALCOATL

of his father is unclear. Quetzalcoatl came to the city of Tula, the capital of the Toltecs, as a mysterious stranger with, as they recorded it, a "craggy face." A pious person, he became known for rejecting human sacrifice, something demanded by all the other deities. As the great "culture-bringer" and inventor, he taught the people about woven textiles, featherwork, jade, gold, cotton, and the arts of dancing, painting, and writing.

On several ancient Mexican artifacts is another strange serpent design which reminds one more of the Indian Nagas than of Quetzalcoatl. The name of this creature has been lost in history.

Psychological Attributes: One who prefers the arts to physical activity.

Magickal Attributes: The arts, metallurgy, fate, culture, learning, organization and order, laws, inventions.

Horned Snake

The Huron Indians of North America had a story of a huge serpent named Oniont. This armored snake had a single horn that could pierce rock. If a person was fortunate enough to find even the tiniest piece of this horn, he or she could cure any human illnesses.

Horned serpents appear frequently in Celtic art. These supernatural creatures are most commonly shown with double ram's horns, rather than a single horn. An engraving of Cernunnos (as Lord of Animals) on the Gundrestrup cauldron[1] shows this deity holding a ram-horned serpent by the neck. The horned serpent was a very important part of Celtic belief. Sometimes the serpent was ram-headed instead of just ram-horned.

A snake-dragon with a snake-like body and head, lion's front legs, a bird's hind feet, and a single horn on the center of its nose is depicted in several Babylonian paint-

CELTIC HORNED SNAKE

ings. The name for this snake-dragon was *mushussu* (furious snake). The Babylonians distinguished three other types of horned snake by the names *musmahhu, usumgallu,* and *basmu.*

Psychological Attributes: One who has learned to work with chakra power.

Magickal Attributes: Cure any illnesses.

The Lamia

Ancient writings refer to the Lamia as a race similar to the Sirens. These creatures prefer dry areas and live in ruined cities, caves, and remote desert areas. The Lamia had the upper body and head of a woman, but the lower body of a serpent. They used a golden comb to comb their hair, and had a liking for the flesh of children. The Lamia was fast, powerful, and used spells to lure victims.

Several creatures were called Lamia in ancient Greek myth. In one tale, the Lamia is a mortal virgin who bore several children to Zeus. In another, she is a creature with a Gorgon-like face who ate children. One story tells how Hermes transformed a serpent of crimson, gold, green, and blue spots into a beautiful maiden. The happiness of this girl was destroyed by the philosopher Apollonius, and she screamed and vanished.

A Christian, Martin of Braga, recorded that Lamias lived in rivers and forests and were devils.[2] Johann Weir wrote a whole book on these creatures, *De Lamiis Liber,* published in 1577.

By the seventeenth century, the Lamia had changed her form from a serpent-woman to a scaly, four-legged creature. The back legs had hoofs while the front had paws. She had a woman's face and breasts, but a man's penis.

Psychological Attributes: One who deliberately lures victims into his or her control.

Magickal Attributes: Not recommended.

Nagas

The Nagas of India are perhaps the most fascinating magickal serpents. Children of the goddess Kadru, they usually appeared as half-snake (cobra), half-human in form and were semi-divine in nature. However, they could appear as totally human; the females did this more often than the males. The Nagas were snake-spirits of both water and land.

The Nagas appear to be of more than one kind, each having a different appearance and coloring. Some of those who dwell in ruins, areas with a depressing atmosphere, or subterranean places have black scales with crimson bands. Their faces have a human look, even to the coloration and hair. However, these Nagas are generally not friendly to humans. They can charm anyone who meets their gaze; they both spit poison and have a poisonous bite. These Nagas are not helpful at all.

Other land Nagas are wise, friendly, and guard sacred places or treasures. They keep the black Nagas in check. These cobra-people can also spit poison, although they do so only in defense. They have golden eyes and green-gold scales with silver triangles down the back.

The Nagas who prefer to live in water of some kind have their lairs deep under a clear, fresh water pool, lake, or river. They usually stay neutral in human affairs, although a sincere petition may gain their aid; they are very curious about humans. The water Nagas are the most colorful of this serpent species. Their scales range in color from emerald green to turquoise; they are often patterned with colors from deep brown and pale jade green to dark gray and olive green. Their eyes range in hue from pale green to bright amber. Even though their bite and saliva are venomous, these Nagas prefer to use magick spells.

The Nagas could cause or prevent rain, and had great powers and wealth. The Nagas had power, positive and negative, over all water, including the rivers and seas. Myth says they gained their semi-divine status when the gods and demons churned the seas to create the magickal soma. During the struggle between the gods and demons over this soma, a few drops splashed onto the ground. The Nagas quickly lapped it up, but there was not enough to grant them total divinity.

The Nagas are said to live in a land which lies either under water or under the Earth. Their capital city and principal home is the underground kingdom called Bhagavati (rich in treasure), probably located deep under the Himalayas. There, it is said, they have beautiful palaces decked in rich gems and precious metals. The streets are paved with mosaics of emeralds, rubies, sapphires, and other colorful gems. The Nagas also keep books of great mystical knowledge.[3] In the throat or forehead of every Naga is a precious jewel of unmeasurable value, which gives them their supernatural powers.

Nagini is the name for a female Naga. These serpent-women are very beautiful and wise. There are many tales of them falling in love with and marrying human princes. A Cambodian legend says that the union between a Nagini and a prince founded that country. The Nagas are depicted in sculpture and decoration all around the ancient city of Angkor. Pairs of Nagas guarded the entrances to the temples, palaces, and shrines, their seven-headed forms arching over anyone who entered.

As late as the thirteenth century a golden tower stood within the palace grounds. At the top of this tower was a special room where, it was said, the king went each night to sleep. The people believed that it was the home of a nine-headed Nagini who ruled Cambodia through the king. If she failed to appear, the king would die; if he failed to sleep there for even one night, disaster would fall upon the land.

One Nagini deity still worshipped today in India is the Naga Kanya, goddess of the three realms. She is the guardian of underwater treasures and spiritual attainments. The upper part of her body is that of a woman, while the lower part is that of a water serpent. However, over her head arches the form

NAGA KANYA

of a five-headed cobra, signifying Kanya's spiritual powers. She has wings attached to her shoulderblades and a precious jewel in her forehead. In her hands she holds a conch shell, presenting her willingness to pour out blessings upon those who seek her wisdom.

Although most Nagas are both good and bad, a few of their race have performed great deeds and become enlightened. The Naga Sesha lived so virtuous a life that the god Brahma finally granted him immortality. Sesha is now said to support the universe. The god Vishnu sleeps on Sesha's coils, under the shade of his seven heads.

When the Buddha was born, the Nagas sprinkled scented water over him. After Buddha became enlightened, he stayed in meditation for several weeks. His extreme piety attracted the Naga Muchalinda (sometimes spelled Musilinda), a many-headed cobra. Muchalinda formed a resting place with his coils beneath the Buddha as a seat and sheltered the man with his great hood against storms so the Buddha could meditate undisturbed. When the Buddha died, one of the shrines built to honor his memory was in the land of the Nagas.

At least one of their race is not so benevolent toward humans. The demon Naga-Sanniya causes nightmares about snakes.

Some tribes in India still claim descent from the Nagas and honor their ancestors, leaving offerings at certain pools and streams. In Hindu mythology, snakes are connected with the Element of Water and the seas. They are also said to be able to confer invisibility on acceptable humans when these people enter any water.

The Nagas also gave protection to doors and thresholds as well as kept guard over treasure, both physical and spiritual. Doors, thresholds,[4] and treasure, whether physical or spiritual, are considered dangerous things for unprepared humans. The Nagas will only reveal and allow access to these areas if the humans have been found worthy and prepared.

Psychological Attributes: Positive—One who sincerely seeks spiritual treasure. Negative—A person who can charm others into doing anything, but has the nasty habit of spitting poisonous rumors and gossip.

Magickal Attributes: Finding riches of the spirit; the hidden treasure in spiritual seeking, found only by those who are sincere. When faced with calamity and harsh problems, ask the Nagas to help you understand where you strayed from your spiritual path. Helpful Nagas will sometimes help you find buried treasure, win contests and lotteries, or enjoy similar windfalls. Only sincerity will gain their assistance.

Other Indian Serpents

Ananta the Infinite was called the Serpent-Mother by the Hindus. She also had the title of Sarparajni (Serpent Queen). During the times between incarnations of Vishnu and other deities, these gods slept in the coils of Ananta.[5] Ananta is similar to the Egyptian goddess Mehen the Enveloper; Mehen was a great Underworld serpent who cradled the Sun god Ra each night.

The serpent-goddess Kadru, the aunt of the bird-man Garuda, is said to have given birth to all the cobras or cobra-people in India.[6] In ancient Babylon, there was a similar goddess whose name was Kadi of Der; she had a woman's head and breasts attached to the body of a snake. Her children were like the Indian Nagas: human from the waist up.

Psychological Attributes: A person who will be nice one moment and a "snake in the grass" the next.

Magickal Attributes: Very dangerous and unpredictable.

Other Magickal Snakes

The Celtic goddess Brigit had a magickal serpent companion who slept through the winter and came out of its hole on the first day of spring. Brigit was an important figure in Celtic religion. We do know that Brigit had a snake[7] festival in which she was worshipped as a Serpent Goddess, but all evidence of actual happenings was destroyed in the Christian purges of Ireland's Celtic literature. Brigit herself was so firmly rooted in the Celtic consciousness, however, that the Christians had no choice but to turn her into an acceptable saint. The story of Saint Patrick running all the snakes out of Ireland probably refers to the Christians driving out the Druids (who called themselves "serpents") and destroying the Pagan rites of Brigit. The Gaelic charms said for protection against snake bite are remarkably similar to those recited by the Hindus.

An ancient Egyptian story of a fabulous serpent is contained on a fragment of papyrus from the Twelfth Dynasty. This creature is described as having a fifty-foot long body covered with golden scales. The face was a blue-green mask made of lapis lazuli with a three-foot-long golden beard. When it moved, there was a thunder-like sound and the ground shook like an earthquake.

Psychological Attributes: Learning to balance chakra power and study with the necessities of everyday living.

Magickal Attributes: Healing through knowledge of the chakras.

Rainbow Serpent

Australia, West Africa, and parts of North America are the places where the Rainbow Serpent lives. This enormous reptile is always connected with creation and rain-making.

The Rainbow Serpent is known in every part of Australia, where it is called by several names: Karia, Muit, Wulungu, Yulung-gul, and Julunggul. Aborigine legend says that in the early days of creation the Rainbow Serpent's task was to create creeks, rivers, lakes, and waterholes so humans and animals could have water.

RAINBOW SERPENT

Through Yulunggul's interaction with the Wawalag Sisters, sacred places were also created.

When the brilliant arches of rainbows are seen stretching from one water source to another, the Rainbow Serpent is said to be traveling about the country.

The Voodoo mythology of Haiti, which originally came from Africa, has a powerful serpent deity called Damballa. The deity is often thought to appear as a great snake arching across the sky. His consort Ayida is the rainbow itself. Entwined in the form of the rainbow, these creatures symbolize sexual unity.

Psychological Attributes: A person who practices sexual and procreative responsibility.

Magickal Attributes: Rain, procreation, magick, life, blood.

Serpents of Sheba

Arab traditions tell of a strange race of serpents called the Serpents of Sheba. These snakes, colored royal purple, were said to live in or near the Moon temple at Marib in Sheba. Instead of creeping about the ground, these sacred serpents lived in trees.[8]

Not much information remains about these Serpents of Sheba. We do know they were held to be very sacred. No one could molest or harm them.

Psychological Attributes: One who has learned that true power comes from the spiritual or Tree of Life.

Magickal Attributes: Learning Moon magick; working with intense Goddess energies.

White Snake of China

The White Snake of Hangchow, China, was essentially an evil creature. For thousands of years she lived in a mountain cave, worshipping the Sun and Moon; she also practiced the most rigid austerities until she became extremely powerful. The White Snake delighted in causing all kinds of calamities for humans. Finally, she assumed the form of a beautiful woman and married a human male. When the husband eventually discovered her true nature, he went to a Buddhist abbot, who used his spiritual powers to trap the White Snake in a small box and bury her under the Pagoda of Thunder and Wind at Hangchow Lake.

Manasa Devi, a snake-goddess of India, was just as ruthless as the White Snake. However, she could be generous if humans let her have her way.

Psychological Attributes: A demanding person who wants his or her way in all things.

Magickal Attributes: Too dangerous.

Winged Serpent

The Winged Serpent is probably the most ancient and commonly pictured fabulous winged snake. Aristotle wrote of Winged Serpents found in India, saying they were nocturnal and noxious. Virgil, Ovid, Lucan, and other ancient writers knew of and wrote about Winged Serpents; however, Herodotus said they were found only in Arabia. Josephus recorded that flying serpents frequently infested the lands which bordered the Nile. Cicero saw Egyptian ibises killing and eating winged snakes that came into Egypt from Libya.

Winged Serpents are familiar creatures in ancient Egyptian art. Some sculptures show them with two or four wings; the wings do not have feathers, but are like those of bats. These creatures were said to guard the trees which produced frankincense, a sacred incense.

Ua Zit (also known as Iusaset or Per-Uatchet) was an ancient Serpent-Mother of Egypt; the Greeks called her Buto. Often Buto is shown winged and/or crowned. Myths say she helped Isis protect her infant son Horus by placing him on the floating island of Chemnis.

Her material symbol in Egyptian art is the uraeus (cobra). The Pyramid Texts call her the Celestial Serpent who gives the food which confers eternal life.[9] In Arabic, the words for snake, life, and teaching are all related. Ua Zit, or Buto, is often shown as a winged cobra over or near the pharaoh; her primary duty was to protect this ruler.

Buto's sacred books of magick were kept in a crypt under the Egyptian god Thoth's main temple at Hermopolis Magna in Upper Egypt. These texts were available to only the disciples of this tem-

BUTO (WINGED SERPENT)

ple. Later races translated these books into the works of Hermes Trismegistus and the Kybalion (not to be confused with the Jewish Qabala). The most secret part of the temple of Thoth was said to be hidden in an underwater palace, which was guarded by an immortal serpent.[10]

Another Egyptian Underworld serpent was the terrible Apep. Each night as the Sun passed through his realm, Apep tried to swallow it. Apep was said to live both deep in the Nile and in the Abyss (the Egyptian Underworld) and was considered to be the deadly enemy of the gods. He had tough, scaly skin, a poisonous bite, and could breathe fire. Apep was usually accompanied by five to fifty other serpents who carried out his will.

The Egyptian Book of the Dead is full of serpent-demons, besides Apep. These demon-snakes are shown spitting fire, sometimes winged, rearing up or standing on legs, and armed with knives.

In medieval alchemy, Apep became known as the Apophis-snake, a hidden spirit who could reveal the secret of the Philosopher's Stone.

Other cultures also knew of giant serpents, who could destroy the world if not controlled. Among these were Koshchei the Death-less of the Russian Underworld;[11] Koshi, the Japanese serpent-dragon of the sea-tides;[12] and the Greek sea serpent of the outermost ocean, Oceanos (Oceanus). The Middle Eastern deity Ahriman was often called the Great Serpent, leader of the Zoroastrian devils.

Mertseger was the snake goddess of the Egyptian Theban necropolis and protected the desert tombs in the Valley of the Kings. She is portrayed in a painting from one of these tombs, dating from the New Kingdom period (1738–1102 B.C.E.).

Psychological Attributes: Positive—Learning how to tap into chakra power to raise one's self spiritually. Negative—Deliberately or subconsciously creating a negative atmosphere, usually because of jealousy or for revenge.

Magickal Attributes: Apep—Darkness, storms, the night, the Underworld, death. Buto—Protection; hiding from evil; teaching. Serpent of Thoth—Guide into the presence of Thoth and his wisdom and ancient knowledge. Ahriman—Not recommended.

Zaltys

In the eastern Baltic countries lived a small, non-venomous snake called the Zaltys. The Zaltys was said to look like an ordinary little green snake, with no wings and nothing extraordinary about it. It was a non-aggressive, fortune-bringing little creature, considered sent by the gods to families. If a Zaltys was seen on a farm, the people were careful not to offend it. They set out saucers of milk, and often tried to tempt it to live inside the house. A Zaltys was said to bring prosperity and good luck.

As a divine watchdog, the Zaltys kept an eye on the family's morals. If the family with whom it lived became greedy or showed other questionable morals, the little snake would simply glide silently away, taking the family's prosperity and luck with it.

Psychological Attributes: One who has learned the negative and positive power words have upon life.

Magickal Attributes: A type of divine watchdog who can bring prosperity and good luck.

ENDNOTES

1. This ancient silver cauldron was found in 1891 in Denmark, at Gundrestrup, in Jutland. Anne Ross. *The Pagan Celts.*

2. John Holland Smith. *The Death of Classical Paganism.*

3. Mark Tatz and Jody Kent. *Rebirth.*

4. Doors and thresholds, especially those of temples and sacred places, have long been considered to symbolize the door and threshold into deep areas of powerful spiritual knowledge.

5. Wendy Doniger O'Flaherty. *Hindu Myths.*

6. Ibid.

7. Sometimes this serpent is called a dragon when associated with Brigit.

8. J. Oliver Thomson. *History of Ancient Geography.*

9. Jack Lindsay. *The Origins of Astrology.*

10. Gaston Maspero. *Popular Stories of Ancient Egypt.*

11. W. R. Lethaby. *Architecture, Mysticism & Myth.*

12. Gertrude and James Jobes. *Outer Space.*

14

The Riddling Sphinx

The Sphinx of Egypt, Greece, or other cultures has always fascinated humans. As with other magickal, mythical creatures, a part of us remembers that the Sphinx has a much deeper meaning than is known or given today.

Egyptian Sphinx

The image of the Egyptian Sphinx is familiar because of the badly eroded Egyptian monument near the pyramids. This ancient statue is a gigantic rock carving just outside Gaza, Egypt, of the reclining body of a lion with an apparently male human head. Today, the Sphinx is eroded and damaged, a far cry from its once-great beauty. When Islam gained control over Egypt, a fanatical Moslem deliberately broke off the nose, calling the statue a sinful idol.

131

To the ancient Egyptians, who called it *hu*[1] (hewn thing), it symbolized the four Elements plus spirit, and all the science of the past now lost to us. Although it crouches not far from the Great Pyramid, the Sphinx was built much later than this famous structure.

The Sphinx of Egypt was of a different type than the one of Greece. The Egyptian Sphinx was considered to be male, because it wore a long headdress falling to its shoulders, was wingless, and wore the royal uraeus (cobra). However, many ancient writers knew the Sphinx to be an androgynous being, an entity holding both masculine (positive) and feminine (negative) creative powers.[2] The Egyptian Sphinx, a regal but enigmatic creature, seems to have been a guardian of the Underworld, that Otherworld realm spoken of by initiates as the place of the great initiations.

The Egyptian Sphinx is almost seventy feet high and over two hundred feet long; its weight is estimated to be hundreds of tons. Originally it probably had a covering of plaster painted in sacred colors. The Sphinx was, outwardly, a representation of the Sun god and adorned with the royal headdress, a cobra (uraeus) on its forehead, and a beard on its chin. Both the cobra and the beard were broken off at some time; the beard was discovered between the front paws when the Sphinx was excavated from its covering of sand.

The main body of the Sphinx is carved from one gigantic stone, with the front paws made of smaller stones. There has been much debate about whether the stone was a huge native rock. An analysis of the limestone has found vast numbers of small sea creatures embedded in it, which points to a strong possibility that the main stone may have been quarried somewhere else.

The temple, the altar between the paws, and the steps leading up to the Sphinx were built at a much later date, probably by the Romans, who restored many Egyptian monuments.

There is a huge red granite stele between its front paws, which has hieroglyphs stating that the Sphinx is a guardian.[3] Some of the hieroglyphs on this stele record the strange vision-dream had by Thuthmosis IV of the Eighteenth Dynasty as he slept in the shadow of the Sphinx. Thuthmosis was, at the time of the dream, still a prince. Growing tired while on a hunting expedition, the prince lay down to sleep in the shade of this ancient statue. He dreamed that the Sphinx asked him to clear away the entrapping sand and restore its magnificence. In return, it would reward Thuthmosis with the double crown of Egypt. Obviously, Thuthmosis honored this request

EGYPTIAN SPHINX

(although the part of the stele which records this is too badly damaged to read), for he became the pharaoh Thuthmosis IV.

Conservative archaeologists, historians, and scholars are determined in their belief that the Sphinx was carved in the image of a great pharaoh as a funerary offering. However, ancient historical sources, ignored by these "experts," give a different story of the use of the Sphinx.

Iamblichus wrote that the Egyptian Sphinx covered the entrance to sacred subterranean chambers and galleries where initiates underwent certain trials. A huge bronze gate sealed the door into the Sphinx, and the method of its opening was known only to certain high priests and priestesses. The confusing maze of hallways within the Sphinx would lead the initiate back to the beginning unless he or she was fully and truly prepared. Once on the right path, much like going through a maze, the way led from ritual chamber to ritual chamber. Only if the initiate was found to be ready for the greatest initiation was he or she guided to the deeper tunnel which led from the Sphinx, under the sand and into the Great Pyramid itself.

George Hunt Williamson said that these underground temples still hold ancient tablets of precious metals, rolls of papyri, and clay tablets recording ancient information.

To disprove ancient writers, metal rods have been driven into the Sphinx throughout the years; no chambers or passages were found within the body. However, in October 1994, the Associated Press reported that workers trying to repair damage to the Sphinx made a fantastic discovery: an unknown ancient passage which leads deep inside the Sphinx. As yet, the antiquities experts do not know who built this passage, where it leads, or what its purpose was.

Sometimes the Sphinx was portrayed with a hawk-head instead of a human one. Egyptian Sphinxes always recline. Often a pair of Sphinx statues were placed to guard the entrance to a temple.

However, images of Sphinxes have been found in cultures older than Egypt. In Mesopotamia, stone carvings of these creatures have been dated to at least 5,000 years older than the Sphinx at Gaza. Other similar carvings have been uncovered throughout the Near East. Even the ancient Greeks had a legend about the Sphinx.

Greek Sphinx

The Greek Sphinx always had the head and breasts of a woman and was winged. She was aggressive, voluble, and predatory, with a liking for human flesh. The word Sphinx comes from the Greek *sphiggein*

(to bind tight; strangle).

The Theban Sphinx is the best known of Greek Sphinxes. She had the head and breasts of a woman, the body of a lion, the clawed feet of a lion, the tail of a dragon, and the wings of a bird. Not much is known of her origin, although one legend says she was the offspring of Typhon and Echidna, while another said she was the child of Orthos and the Chimera. Her favorite spot was on a rock beside the road leading into the city of Thebes,

GREEK SPHINX

where she challenged all travelers with a riddle she learned from the Muses. Those who could not give the correct answer were destroyed; Oedipus finally answered the riddle correctly.

Remaining legends say that the Greek Sphinx occasionally walked around the countryside from place to place. Tradition also notes several flight-paths taken by the Sphinx between various Greek islands.

The Grecian Sphinx liked to talk to and torment her victims before killing them. If a victim did manage to escape, her rage was terrible. Jung compared this creature to the archetypal Terrible Mother. The throne of Zeus at Olympia had a design of Sphinxes carrying off children. These pictures may have been symbolic of the connection between Zeus and the Sphinx, who may have carried out the god's orders for retribution.

Other Sphinxes

The earliest Assyrian, Persian, and Phoenician Sphinxes were male and had beards and long curly hair. However, after the seventh century B.C.E., winged female Sphinxes appeared in the Assyrian carvings. In ancient Phoenicia, both male and female Sphinxes were portrayed. The Hittites carved rock images of lion bodies with human heads. Like the Grecian Sphinx, the Sphinx of Babylon was female. Legends say that the Middle Eastern Sphinxes had great wisdom, rarely revealed their knowledge, and were content to be honored by humans.

The Roman Sphinx was female and wore an uraeus on her forehead. She probably took her feminine form from the Greek Sphinx, but many other attributes from the Sphinx of Egypt. Strangely enough, images of the Sphinx have also been found among the Mayan ruins of the Yucatan.

All the Sphinxes can speak all languages known now, or in ancient times, to humans. Sphinxes have learned every form of magick ever known and forgotten by humans. They are adept at using magick spells. They also prize gems in all forms, precious metals, and books, especially ancient ones.

In general, the male of this species is larger than the female and more powerful in physical strength. When angry or issuing a challenge, the deafening roar of the male Sphinx can be heard for many miles.

The female of the species is actually more intelligent than the male, but the males are also extremely wise and knowledgeable. The female Sphinx is more apt to help humans with poetry, prose, riddles, and general knowledge.

The Sphinx is a reminder that humans have spiritual wings, human heads (or minds), and beast bodies. As the guardian of the sacred ancient Mysteries, the Sphinx crouches before the gates of the superconscious mind and denies entrance to those not qualified to enter. Meeting a Sphinx heralds a time of spiritual growth and even a possible new love.

Psychological Attributes: Positive—A person who knows when to keep silent and when to speak. Negative—One who likes to challenge people on intellectual levels, then verbally tear them to pieces if they prove to be "less" intelligent. A person who practices "one-up-manship."

Magickal Attributes: Initiation, end of a cycle. Elemental magick. Meeting the Dark Mother; instruction from Her. The Roman and Greek Sphinxes were symbols of violent natures and wanton destruction. The Greeks associated their Sphinx with initiation and death. A mysterious magickal creature, the Sphinx was said to possess the deepest secrets of the universe, but remained eternally silent.

ENDNOTES

1. Manly Hall gives the Egyptian word as *hu* while Max Thoth lists it as *uh*.
2. Gerald Massey in 1883 came to this same conclusion.
3. Max Thoth gives the interpretation of several lines of these hieroglyphs.

15

Mad Dogs and Hell Hounds

Dogs have always been associated with the Underworld, the Moon, and the deities, especially goddesses, of death and divination. There is still a folk belief that dogs will howl when there is a death in the family to whom the dogs belong. A magician must take extreme care in what type of magickal dog he or she calls upon, as a great many of them are dangerous.

Dogs symbolize the dark side or forces of each human personality, which can rear its head from time to time in life. Since these forces are an integral part of the personality, there is no way we can completely eradicate them. However, we can, and should, learn how to keep them under conscious control.

The Black Dog

In Scotland and Ireland, the dreaded Black Dog has been seen over the centuries by many people. Due to the widespread emigration of Celtic peoples, the Black Dog has made appearances in many parts of the world. People of Celtic descent do not like to walk lonely roads without a companion, especially at night. Although the companion may never see this spectral creature, he or she does offer some protection from it.

This supernatural creature is almost always considered to be a dangerous omen, but in rare instances has been helpful to those who see it. Tradition says that if one speaks to or strikes at the Black Dog, the creature has the power to blast.[1] This "blast" consists of first harming the person mentally, then causing a physical decline which may lead to death. Sometimes the Black Dog appears as an instrument of divine justice, stalking a guilty person until justice is achieved in one form or another.[2]

Tradition says that the best companion is a descendant of Ean MacEndroe of Loch Ewe. Clan history tells us that, in the year of Culloden, a Faery granted Ean MacEndroe and all his descendants protection from the power of the Black Dog. Ean found the Faery tangled in a bramble bush and released her. In gratitude, the Faery bestowed upon him this protection.

Descriptions of the Black Dog are often vague, basically because of the deep and lasting fear which it engenders. This ghostly creature's appearance also fills the viewer with a chilly despair and despondency, followed by a decline in vitality. Some say the Black Dog is shaggy and as big as a calf, while others say it is no larger than a Labrador dog. All viewers, however, agree that it has huge fiery eyes and makes absolutely no sound: no panting, no clicking of toenails. If the watcher yells at the specter or makes any noise, the Black Dog pays no attention.

This frightening apparition does not generally attack or chase anyone. It just follows and projects its aura of deadly fear, which is enough to cause some viewers to become very ill afterward. As a death omen, the Black Dog is harmless unless touched; then the person is said to die.

One particular Scottish clan has good reason to fear the appearance of the Black Dog to any of their members. Whenever any member of the Clan MacLartin sees this creature, it is a prophecy of an ignoble death "on a dunghill," so the story goes. The last member to see the Black Dog was Lord Jamie MacLartin in 1715. A few days after it followed Jamie, English dragoons hung him and threw his body on a dunghill.

On the moors and wastelands of the Scottish and northern English countryside there is a legend of a similar black dog called Black Angus. It is said this animal appears to those who are destined to die within a short time. In the English district of East Anglia there is a tradition of a great black, fiery-eyed dog called Shuck, who is also an apparition of evil.

The Church Grim is another type of Black Dog, a great spectral dog that guards churchyards from demon-spirits and malicious people. Those who see the Church Grim considered it to be a death warning. The area of Somerset seems to have an extraordinary number of stories about Church Grims. Stories of the Yorkshire Church Grim report that this creature can be seen in and about the church, day or night, during storms. It has been known to ring the bells at midnight before someone in the parish dies. Several of the older clergymen reported seeing this dog looking down from the tower during funerals.

BLACK DOG

CERBERUS

Psychological Attributes: A person who always sees the worst in every situation and never fails to tell everyone who will listen.

Magickal Attributes: Most commonly a bad or death omen and not to be called upon in magick, except for divine justice on those who have escaped punishment.

Cerberus

The great Underworld hound Cerberus (Spirit of the Pit)[3] guarded the entrance to the Greek afterlife, the realm of Hecate, Persephone, and Hades. It was a monstrous dog with three mastiff heads, sometimes with the tail of a serpent or dragon. For the souls of the dead to enter the Underworld, they had to present Cerberus with gifts of honey and barley cakes. It was the job of Cerberus to keep out living humans who might try to rescue loved ones from the Underworld. One of the few living humans to enter and leave this realm successfully was Orpheus, who played sweet music on his lyre. As one of the labors appointed by the gods, Heracles had to drag Cerberus to the city of Tiryns.

Certain herbs were believed to have been infected with the venom of Cerberus' saliva. These herbs were gathered and used by some magicians for evil spells.

Although Cerberus was associated with Greece and the Mediterranean area, a painted linen panel from Tibet also shows a many-headed dog.

Psychological Attributes: Often a person who has learned to work with the terminally ill and dying.

Magickal Attributes: Contacting specific departed souls for information and help.

Coyote

A Native American magickal creature, Coyote has the form of a larger-than-life, but otherwise ordinary coyote. He is known primarily as a bullying, greedy, untrustworthy trickster being. He was, however, also the creature who taught humans about the arts, crafts, and the use of fire. In his trickster aspect, Coyote is sometimes accompanied by a giant wolf, fox, wildcat, badger, or porcupine. Even though he is an intelligent being, his tricks more often than not backfire on him. His two strongest powers are to become invisible and the ability to move things from one place to another, himself included.

Psychological Attributes: One who likes to stir up trouble, then stand back and watch; sometimes a thief.

Magickal Attributes: Although a powerful energy force, also devious and dangerous. Invisibility. The breaking free of negative power from the universal order of things, causing chaos.

Cu Sith

The fearsome Cu Sith [coo-shee] roamed the Scottish Highlands. He was an enormous, shaggy, dark green hound, as big as a bullock, with a braided tail and feet as big as those of humans.[4] Although the Cu Sith was a creature belonging to, and controlled by, the Faeries, it was very different from the ordinary Faery hounds, which were white with red ears. It only bayed three times when hunting. Footprints of the Cu Sith have been seen in mud or snow, in a straight line across the countryside.

However, anyone who actually sees the Cu Sith reports that it glides silently, never making a sound except for its terrible baying. Its deep baying can be heard over the dark moors as he goes out in search of human women to drive into the Faery mounds; these women become the nursemaids for Faery children.

Psychological Attributes: One who enjoys using magick or psychic experiences to frighten others.

Magickal Attributes: Dangerous, but can help make contact with the Faery realm.

Fenris

Fenris was a giant wolf in Norse mythology, a child of Angrboda by Loki. His name is sometimes given as Fenrir. Snorri gives the alternative name Vanargandr (the guardian monster of the river Van).

Norse myth says that Fenris became so dangerous that the gods decided he had to be permanently restrained. They tried two

FENRIS

magickally reinforced chains, but nothing could keep the great wolf from breaking them. Finally, the Dwarves forged the chain Gleipnir, which was made of such things as the roots of a mountain, the mew of a cat, and a fish's breath. Fenris was too wily to submit tamely to being bound with this chain; he insisted that the god Tyr put his right hand into his mouth. When Fenris found he could not break this chain, he bit off the god's hand.

Fenris was taken to the island of Lyngvi, in the middle of the lake Amsvartnir (the completely black one). The fetter-chain around Fenris was fastened to a chain called Gelgja, which in turn was chained to a great rock called Gjoll.

Although Fenris is chained to prevent the destruction he might cause, Norse myth says he will break free at the end of the world. This end-of-the-world event is called Ragnarok, the Day of the Wolf.

Psychological Attributes: A person who is a potential powderkeg; the slightest relaxation of your guard around him or her might put you in danger. Abusers fall into this category.

Magickal Attributes: Fenris can be useful when you need to harness destructive forces that are destroying your life. However, this energy is very dangerous; should it, even for a moment, get out of your control, you will feel the backlash of the negative side of Fenris.

Garm

This Norse supernatural dog or wolf was sometimes said to lead the pack in the Wild Hunt and lived in the goddess Hel's Underworld realm. His name is also translated as Managarm or Garmr (Moon Dog), according to the *Prose Edda*. Garm's primary duty was to guard the gates leading into Hel's kingdom, both to keep unauthorized people out and deceased souls in. His howls were hair-raising.

The *Voluspa* records that Garm was chained at Gnipahellir (overhanging cave) at the entrance to Hel's realm. At Ragnarok, legend says, he will break free and take part in the great battle against the gods.

Garm looks like a giant menacing wolf, a prehistoric creature of great ferocity and strength, with a large head. Usually, just seeing this chthonic dog-wolf is enough to make humans run in terror. Although Garm's usual place is at the gates of Hel's realm, he does travel to the physical plane with the goddess when she is gathering souls of deceased humans. Whenever this giant dog-wolf travels, he is accompanied by a pack of creatures that look just like him, but are smaller in size. When Hel is journeying away from her kingdom, accompanied by Garm, the gates to her Underworld are sealed.

Another of Garm's duties is to guard the island where Fenris is chained.

Psychological Attributes: One who resists any attempt to control the dark side of his or her personality, but who enjoys the feeling of fear engendered by the dark side.

Magickal Attributes: Very dangerous; not recommended except by experienced magicians seeking a better rapport with the Crone aspect of the Goddess or the Lord of Darkness. A magician who understands and uses Crone power to right wrongs.

Geri and Gifr

According to the Fjolsvinnsmal, Geri (the greedy one) was one of the hounds of hell that protected the goddess Hel. The other personal bodyguard of Hel was Gifr (the noisy one, screamer).

Geri was also the name of one of the wolves of Odhinn, listed in the *Grimnismal*. The other wolf was called Freki (Voracious). These two wolves accompanied Odhinn everywhere and did the god's bidding. They were fed from the tables in Odhinn's hall in Valhalla.

Psychological Attributes: The wild, deeply buried part of your subconscious which can break out under stress and cause you grief and regrets.

Magickal Attributes: Although protective and messengers from the gods, these wolf-dog powers are very dangerous.

Hati and Skoll

Hati (despiser, hater) is named in the *Grimnismal* as the son of Hrodvitnir. He was a wolf who ran in front of the Sun, chasing the Moon. At Ragnarok, Hati will catch and devour the Sun. Skoll (mockery), the second wolf, ran before the Moon, chasing the Sun. He will catch and devour the Moon at Ragnarok.

Psychological Attributes: One who deliberately tries to tear down or destroy the lives of others.

Magickal Attributes: Very dangerous; retribution for those who persecute or harass you.

The Heaven Dog

The "Heaven Dog" of China is called T'ien Kou [tea-en go]. He is said to be both benevolent and terrible. When he is in his yang energy, he helps the god Erh-lang drive off evil spirits; in this aspect he represents fidelity and devotion. However, during the night he is in his yin energy and represents destruction and catastrophe.

This celestial dog was said to have descended from the skies and was a terrifying creature. He liked to feed on newborn children, and was an omen of destruction and disaster. As the meteor demon, he tries to devour the Sun, thereby causing solar eclipses. When he bites the Moon, he causes comets, meteors, and lunar eclipses.

Sixth-century B.C.E. records mention one of the first appearances of the T'ien Kou. He came to Earth like a comet with a long

HEAVEN DOG

tail of fire; this light appeared over thousands of miles and poisoned all the crops where it fell. The emperor was terrified; he tried to propitiate this dog-like creature by covering several acres with human livers. The entire populace of the capital barricaded themselves in their homes until the emperor managed to drive away the T'ien Kou without human sacrifices.

Although there is said to be more than one T'ien Kou, only one such creature appears at a time, and then only on rare occasions. Such an appearance is always considered to be a portent of calamity. Sometimes the T'ien Kou is said to be connected with a great star in or near the constellation of Cancer, the same great White Star which foretells war and disaster in Japan.

In the second century the T'ien Kou was said to appear in the shape of a gigantic shooting star, making a terribly loud noise. He is always accompanied by thunder. One of the Taoist deities, the "Immortal Chang," or Chang Hsien, had only one function: to drive away the T'ien Kou. He was said to do this by shooting at this creature with a bow made of mulberry wood. Dog hair, worn as an amulet, protects against the T'ien Kou.

An early twentieth-century Chinese drawing shows the celestial dog-demon with four clawed feet, spots or tufts of hair all over its body and around its head, and the tail as a mass of long flowing hair.

Psychological Attributes: Positive—One who uses psychic predictive abilities to help others. Negative—A person who revels in revealing unsettling and negative predictions.

Magickal Attributes: Protection and exorcism of evil spirits; fidelity. If the Heaven Dog appears as an omen of destruction and catastrophe, call upon the Immortal Chang to repel him.

Hounds of the Wild Hunt

The Wild Hunt or Ride of Death appears in many forms throughout Europe; in every instance, the Hunt is accompanied by a pack of supernatural hounds. To the Norse and Germanic peoples, this Hunt was led by Odhinn (Anglo-Saxon Wodan) or the Erl King. They were said to appear only in stormy weather and were a death omen to anyone who heard them. The Norse also said that an evil spirit or witch called Lusse took the form of a gigantic bird of prey on the night of December 12–13 and flew with the Hunt, which was then called the Lussiferd or Lussireidi.

The Anglo-Saxon Chronicle of 1127 describes the Wild Hunt. After February 6 of that year, a great many people in England heard and saw a large party of huntsmen and their hounds coursing through the dark night. The huntsmen rode black horses or bucks; their black dogs had fierce staring eyes. Strangely enough, this same spectacle was seen and heard again at Halloween in the 1940s at Taunton, England.

The French had their Grand Huntsman; the Irish their Hell Hounds; the British Celts their Dogs of Annwn or the Underworld. The Hounds of the Wild Hunt were given many names: the Gabriel Hounds, Yeth Hounds, the Devil's Dandy Dogs, the Gabriel Ratchets, Whistlers, the Dartmoor Pack, or the Wisht or Whisht Hounds. Even King Arthur, in one folk tale, was said to ride the stormy night skies with a pack of spectral hounds.

The ancient Greeks believed that dogs were creatures of the Moon goddesses and the Underworld. Their fearsome Erinyes were three women who could take the form of dogs and hunt down those who broke spiritual laws; these frightening beings had snakes twined in their long hair.

The Hounds of the Wild Hunt were known to the Celts as the Hounds of Annwn and to the Norse as the companion-hounds of Hel and Odhinn. The Hounds of Annwn, or the Cwn Annwn [koon anoon], the hunting hounds of the Underworld king Arawn, were pure white with red ears. They were known as death-omen hounds, although they did not cause destruction or chase humans to death. It was said that when they were near they sounded like small dogs, but from a distance their cry was deep, hollow, and wild, like the bay of bloodhounds. Their baying call was also said to get softer as they got nearer. When Arawn or his successor, Gwynn ap Nudd of Wales, rode out on his Hunt, he usually chased a white stag instead of humans.

This Underworld realm, known as Annwn, was not the hell postulated by the Christians; it was merely the realm where all humans went when they died. Although there were dark regions of this realm, there were also vast areas much like the countryside of Britain: thick forests and rolling pastures with bright flowers, mountains, and rivers. Those deceased souls found worthy were invited by Arawn to hunt deer, eat from the magick cauldron which never ran dry, and drink from fountains that poured forth wine.

THE WILD HUNT

The Hounds of the Hill is an English term for the Cwn Annwn, stemming from the belief that Faeries lived in the hollow hills. These hounds are described in the usual way: white with red ears. In both 1917 and 1970, a young laborer befriended a Hound of the Hill, the size of a calf, with a white coat and red ears. He tended its sore feet; then the dog disappeared. At a later date, the young man was attacked in some manner and rescued by the Hound.

In Dartmoor and parts of Cornwall, the spectral Hounds, called Wish Hounds, Yeth-Hounds, or Yell-Hounds, are not as friendly as the Cwn Annwn. These supernatural creatures are said to be headless, and the huntsman either the devil or some human trapped by the devil. The ghost of Sir Francis Drake has been seen driving a hearse through the streets of Plymouth followed by a great pack of similar headless hounds.

An antler-horned Huntsman haunts Windsor Great Park. This being is called Herne the Hunter. He too leads a Wild Hunt and was at one time said to be a conductor of souls to the Underworld.

Because the Christians could not get the people to stop believing in these supernatural creatures, they changed the name of these Hounds to Hell (Hel's) Hounds and said they hunted down the souls of sinners.[5] Stories say that these Hell Hounds, with their fiery eyes, terrible fangs, and savage yelps, would follow the scent of a sinner and never give up until they dragged him or her into the Christian Hell. This Wild Hunt, led by their devil, was sometimes called Herla's Rade, Dando and his dogs, or Cheney's Hounds.

Our word "harlequin" comes in a roundabout way from an Old French version of the Wild Hunt. Originally, the Hellequins or

Herlequins were the women who rode with the goddess Hel on the nightly hunts, but when the idea was taken into the French culture, they changed Hel to a mythical male rider called King Herla (Odhinn), or Herlequin (Old English Herla Cyning). Thus, the English term Herla's Rade.

The Erl King's name can be traced back to the Danish *erlkonig, ellerkonge,* or *elverkonge,* literally "king of the elves." It may well be that the French Hellequin came from the Danish Erl King. The *erlkonig* [earl-koe-neeg] was also part of Germanic folktales, and sometimes was said to warn certain humans about their approaching death. He appeared as a handsome elf, wearing a golden crown and dressed in beautiful clothing adorned with embroidery and fur.

As a kind of counterbalance to the Hell Hounds, the Christians also created what they called the Hounds of Heaven. These creatures hunted down sinners to force them to repent and rejoin the Christian church. If the sinner escaped, then the Hell Hounds were set on their trail. The Heaven Hounds were said to have a cry-like bay, while the Hell Hounds' bay was savage, fading as they drew nearer.

On the moors of West England these hounds were called the Devil's Dandy Dogs. They were described as a pack of fire-breathing, glowing-eyed hounds led by the devil. They appeared on stormy nights and were said to tear anyone they encountered to pieces. In the northern part of England they were known as the Whisht Hounds; legend said they were the souls of unbaptized children. They hunted only on wild nights and were a death omen.

The Devil's Dandy Dogs were the Cornish version of the Hounds of the Wild Hunt. This pack was considered to be the most dangerous of all the supernatural dog packs, for the Cornish devil hunts human souls.

Lewis Spence[6] wrote that the Gabriel Hounds of Lancashire, sometimes called sky-yelpers, were headless and raced high in the skies. If the pack hovered over a house, that family would see a death or misfortune in a short time. Another name for them were the Gabriel Ratchets, "ratchet" being a very old name for a hound which hunts by scent. In the seventeenth century these same hounds were called Lyme Hounds.

Norse mythology tells of the heavenly Moon dogs, the children of the goddess Angrboda; the Underworld goddess Hel was also a child of this goddess. The Moon dogs were huge black hounds with phosphorescent green eyes the size of saucers. During their stormy night hunts, they were followed by the god Odhinn and his ghostly companions.[7]

This description fits many traditions' reports of the Hounds of the Wild Hunt. Often these spectral dogs were said to have lolling, glowing green tongues. These hounds raced before the Wild Hunt, with the rest of the company behind them. The howling and baying of the hounds and the blast of the Huntsman's horn could be heard for miles as they raced through the night skies, often just above the ground. Nothing was an obstacle to their progress.

The greatest danger of seeing this spectral Hunt was that the watcher could get caught up in it, either as part of the Hunters or as the hunted. If the watcher became the prey of the Wild Hunt, the only hope was to elude them until morning, when they would disappear. The watcher, whether part of the Hunters or the hunted, could not break the spell of the Hunt until first light. If the watcher was caught up as part of the Hunters, he or she would be able to keep up, whatever the speed, but could not break the spell to leave the Hunt until morning.

A few legends tell of a person who has fought against the Wild Hunt, hounds and followers, managing to slay some of them, and holding them at bay until first light. When morning came, there was no sign of bodies, and the Wild Hunt reappeared somewhere else the next night.

Psychological Attributes: Positive—One who works with magick to see that violent offenders and those who break laws are punished. Negative—A person who enjoys magickally harming others for what they consider faults.

Magickal Attributes: Hunt down those who break spiritual laws. Seeing and hearing the Hounds of the Hunt is an omen of death or misfortune. However, if the magician has a truthful and pure heart, he or she can be rescued by the Hounds from danger. Erinyes—Retribution for shedding the blood of mothers; justice against those who break social and bloodline laws, such as rape, incest, and murder.

MOON DOGS

Irish Moon Dogs

The old Irish folk tales said that the gates which lead to Emania, the Moon-land, were guarded by two dogs. For this reason, mourners were told not to cry too loudly. Otherwise, the guardian dogs became disturbed and might attack the soul approaching the gate. One of the dogs was named Dormarth (Death's Door).[8]

Psychological Attributes: Learning to work with the terminally ill and dying.

Magickal Attributes: Using Moon magick to contact and learn from departed souls.

Other Spectral Guardian Dogs

Black Dogs have generally been looked upon as sinister, ill-omened creatures, like the Mauthe Doog of Man who menaced people. However, there are a number of stories from the beginning of this century of good-omened Black Dogs, such as the one seen at Birdlip Hill in Gloucestershire. This particular Black Dog was said to guard and guide travelers through the region who either walked the hills alone or traveled the roads at night.

In the northern part of Britain and in Suffolk was a spectral dog known as the Gally-trot, "gally" meaning to frighten. However, this supernatural hound was white instead of black. It was about the size of a calf, although the outline was never quite clear, and would chase anyone who ran from it.

The Faeries are said to have a number of different kinds of dogs for protection and hunting. Among these are the Cu Sith, Cwn Annwn, and the Hounds of the Hill.

ENDNOTES

1. The Mauthe Doog (Black Dog) of Peel Castle in the Isle of Man is feared for this blasting power.
2. Ruth Tongue, in her book *Forgotten Folk-Tales of the English Countries*, tells a story in which the Black Dog does just this.
3. Robert Graves. *Greek Myths*.
4. This description is a common one in the Highlands. J. G. Campbell wrote it down in his *Superstitions of the Scottish Highlands*.
5. Robert Graves. *White Goddess*.
6. Lewis Spence. *The Fairy Traditions in Britain*.
7. Brian Branston. *Gods of the North*.
8. Charles Squire. *Celtic Myth & Legend, Poetry & Romance*.

16

Water-Folk

The human-like creatures of the Element of Water are classified as Undines and are associated with the West; Undine comes from the Latin *unda,* meaning "wave." Their leader is Necksa or Nicksa. Undines have a great degree of control over the course and action of water itself in the physical world, as well as human emotions in the realm of magick.

Although the Mer-People are the most familiar water beings, there are many classes or species of Water-Folk. Ancient philosophers wrote that the Water-Folk, in one form or another, lived in every source of water: springs, fountains, creeks, rivers, lakes, fens or marshes, waterfalls, and seas. Although the Undines or Water-Folk closely resemble humans in general appearance and size, there are smaller versions of this species that live in smaller bodies of water, such as fountains, springs, and little, slow-moving creeks.

Most of the Water-Folk have some humanoid features, although aquatic forms such as scales and webbed feet and hands are also part of their make-up. Most of them can communicate with humans, if they wish, because they are fluent in the human languages in their area.

Those Water-Folk who live in the dripping, foggy marshes, swamps, and fens are human in shape, with arms and legs, but also with sharp teeth, fish-like eyes, tiny scales covering their bodies, and webs between their fingers and toes. Their hair is stringy and dark, like dead, water-slimed pieces of grass. They generally make their appearance on foggy, cloudy days or at night. The Marsh-People are the most unpredictable and tricky Water-Folk, often deliberately leading humans astray in the fog.

The tiny Water-Folk of the fountains, springs, and creeks are small, human-shaped beings with iridescent scales that flash beautiful colors in the sunlight. The younger ones have fish-tails which disappear as they reach adulthood, rather like tadpoles; these children stay in the water until the transformation is complete. The older folk are human-like with arms and legs, and have the ability to propel themselves upward through the fountain spray. Their dancing through the water reminds one of Faeries, although these beings have no wings or fins. The adults often sun themselves along the edges of their watery homes. They are shy around humans but can sometimes be coaxed to help in water divination.

Those beings who live in waterfalls are very beautiful and look much like their smaller relatives in the fountains and springs, but are human-sized. They can flash straight up the falling water, then drift down, twisting and leaping through the spray. Their young, who also have fish-tails until adulthood, play in the pools below the waterfalls. The Undines of the waterfalls seldom help humans, although they have healing knowledge.

Another water being connected with small waterfalls is the Stromkarl, or River-Man. He plays beautiful but sad music on a harp and has a wonderful voice.

The Water-Folk of rivers and fast-moving streams look more like their cousins who live in the seas. Some of them have fish-tails, some do not. They are usually human-sized and quite attractive. However, they are unreliable, often tempting humans into the water to drown. They love to sing as they sit along the banks, combing their hair.

The Lake-Folk are the most human-looking of all the Water-Folk. The webs between their fingers and toes are so slight as to be undetectable. They rarely have scales on their bodies, and their facial features, except for a remote pale beauty, are human-like. These Water-Folk are as much at home on land as they are in the water, often living among humans for periods of time without anyone being the wiser as to their identity. They have powerful knowledge concerning magick, but when working with them a human must be on guard against glamour-spells that will entice the magician into the lake.

Little is known about another species of Water-Folk, as they are extremely shy about being seen by humans. Some of these tiny beings live among the reeds along river banks and the shores of lakes. Others have their homes under lily pads, in little caves among the rocks of streams, or in miniature moss houses under waterfalls.

Humans are best acquainted with the Mer-People of the seas, with whom we have communicated for centuries. The Mer-People are not all of one type; some of them have permanent fish-tails, while others can shape-shift and go onto the land.

All the Water-Folk love to sing. However, some of their voices, especially the voices of those who live in the swamps, can be frightening. Most of them, though, have enticing, beautiful voices. Although the Water-Folk are emotional and influenced by emotions projected by humans, there is actually little that is human about their personalities and outlook on life.

The Water-Folk represent all emotions, positive and negative, found within humans.

Ahuizotl

This is the name of the terrible creature found in the highland lakes of Central America. Descriptions of this dangerous being are vague because it is rare for a human who sees it to survive. The Ahuizotl considers itself to be the owner of all the fishes in the lakes and goes into a rage when the fishermen "steal" its fish by net and line. When its anger is aroused, the Ahuizotl causes great storms by lashing the water with its long tail. Sometimes it will even grab the sides of a boat and tip it over to drown the fishermen.

Psychological Attributes: One who sees danger even when there is none.

Magickal Attributes: Too dangerous; not recommended.

BEN-VARREY

Ben-Varrey

The people who live on the Isle of Man call the being we know as a Mermaid, the Ben-Varrey [bedn varra]. Like other Mermaids, this species of sea creature can enchant and lure humans to their death, but she sometimes shows a much softer side.

Dora Broome[1] recorded a tale in which a fisherman carried a stranded Ben-Varrey back to the sea and, as a reward, was told where to find a treasure. Another delightful story concerns a baby Mermaid who wanted a little human girl's doll so much she stole it. The Mermaid mother scolded the baby and made her return the doll, along with a string of pearls.

One story told of a friendly Ben-Varrey who lived near Patrick. During one fishing season, as the Peel boats fished off Spanish Head, the Mermaid suddenly rose from the water and cried, *"shiaull er thalloo"* (sail to land!). Those fishermen who had learned to trust the advice of this Mermaid immediately raced their boats for shelter. Those who did not heed the warning lost all their tackle, and some lost their lives.

Psychological Attributes: One who is comfortable with ordinary emotions; not allowing extreme emotions by either bottling them up or letting them explode.

Magickal Attributes: Can give protection and favors, but beware of their enchanting powers.

Bunyips

Bunyips are Australian water monsters also known as Kine Pratie, Wowee Wowee, Dongus, and by many other localized names. There appear to be several different species, all of whom live in the swamps and marshes of different parts of that country. Some Bunyips have the flat face of a bulldog and a tail like a fish; others have the long neck and beaked head of an emu and the flowing mane of a sea serpent; still others somewhat resemble humans. However, all the species can be immediately identified by the fact that their feet are turned backward and their faces are hideous. They are rarely seen.

Bunyips make a loud, booming roar which can be heard over long distances. They live in dens made in the banks of rivers, waterholes, or mangrove swamps. When their dens dry up during droughts, the Bunyips burrow deep into the mud to hibernate. It is common for their frightening roars to be heard during or after long periods of rain, but never during a drought.

Psychological Attributes: Being able to make a comfortable home in terrible circumstances.

Magickal Attributes: Rain.

Bunyips

The Ceasg

The Scottish Highland Mermaid was known as the Ceasg [keeask] or *maighdean na tuinne* (maiden of the wave). She had the body of a beautiful woman, but a large tail like that of a young salmon. The Ceasg was a dangerous creature, who, tradition says, could only be overcome by the destruction of her separable soul. This soul did not inhabit her body, but was kept hidden somewhere, like in an egg, a shell, or a box. The idea of this separable soul was also applied in mythology and folklore to many supernatural beings, as well as to certain magicians.[2]

Highland fishermen were willing to overlook the dangerous qualities of the Ceasg and attempt to capture one. Tradition said that if one could catch a Ceasg, she had to grant three wishes. If she lived with the fisherman, his luck would grow. Several famous Scottish pilots claimed descent from the union of a Ceasg and a human man.

Psychological Attributes: Ignoring the spiritual side of life, or keeping it so separate that you do not really benefit from it.

Magickal Attributes: Very dangerous. If the magician is powerful enough, the Ceasg can grant three wishes.

Dinny-Mara

This Merman of the Isle of Man was also called the Dooinney Marrey [dunya mara]. The Dinny-Mara was said to be far less fierce than the average English Merman, and nearly as gentle and friendly as the Irish Merrow. Folk tales say that these beings were good fathers, romping with their babies and giving them presents. This is in sharp contrast to the Cornish tales, especially those from Cury, which tell of a Mermaid fearing that her husband would eat her children if she were delayed in returning home.

The Cornish Mermaids had a more sinister nature. They might grant three wishes if caught, but they always tried, and usually managed, to get their human victim to drown in the sea.

One such story is part of the folklore of Cury, near Lizard Point in Cornwall. A long time ago a fisherman named Lutey was combing the beach for wreckage when he found a Mermaid stranded in a pool by the tide. She offered him three wishes if he would take her back to the sea. As he carried her along, Lutey asked for the power to break witchcraft spells and to command spirits for the good of others, that these powers should descend through his family, and that none of his family should ever want. The Mermaid gave Lutey her comb by which he could summon her from the sea.

When Lutey got near the sea, she began to cast a spell over him to go with her. The fisherman turned and looked back at his cottage, thus breaking the spell. However, the Mermaid hung onto his neck and would not let go until Lutey drew his knife and held the blade between them. The Mermaid leaped into the water and disappeared. Lutey was safe for nine years until one day he was fishing with one of his sons. The same Mermaid appeared beside the boat and called to him. Without a backward glance, Lutey dove into the sea and disappeared forever.

Psychological Attributes: Wishing or working for things or relationships without giving careful consideration to the fact that the granting of such a wish may not be good for you, then whining when you get what you wanted.

Magickal Attributes: Very sinister; dangerous; not recommended.

Gwragedd Annwn

The Gwragedd Annwn [gwrageth anoon] were the Lake Maidens of Welsh legends. Wales has stories of a great many sinister Faery creatures; the Lake Maidens were not of this type, nor were they like the Sirens or Nixies. They were beautiful and sometimes married mortals. Like Mer-People everywhere, they liked to sit along the banks of their watery home and comb their long hair.

One of the earliest tales about the Gwragedd Annwn is the story of the lady of Llyn y Fan Fach, a small lake near the Black Mountains in Wales. In the twelfth century, a young farm lad from Blaensawde near Mydfai saw and fell in love with a Lake Maiden he watched combing out her long golden hair. He married her, but the lady warned him never to strike her even in jest, for if he struck her three times, she would return to the lake. They lived happily for several years during which she bore three sons. But the man forgot and on three occasions gave her a love-tap. At the last tap, the lady returned to her mountain lake. However, she frequently came to visit her three sons, teaching them the deep secrets of medicine. These boys became the famous physicians of Mydfai. This skill, handed down to them by their Lake Maiden mother, descended in the family until the bloodline died out in the nineteenth century.

Psychological Attributes: Gentleness with an inner strength that enables one to walk away from unpleasant situations.

Magickal Attributes: Deep secrets of healing and medicine.

GWRAGEDD ANNWN

Hai Ho Shang

In the South China Sea, Chinese sailors once feared the Hai Ho Shang (sea Buddhist priest), or sea bonze. This creature was described as having a large fish-body and the shaven head of a Buddhist priest. Stories say that the Hai Ho Shang was aggressive and strong, so strong that it could seize and capsize fishing boats, drowning the entire crew. However, there were two known methods for repelling this sea creature. The crew could burn feathers, or someone could perform a set ritual dance. It became common for at least one Chinese sailor on each junk to be trained in these protective ritual steps, besides his regular duties.

Psychological Attributes: Overly aggressive and uncaring when it comes to getting what you want.

Magickal Attributes: Dangerous; not recommended.

Hippocampus

This sea creature was considered a prize steed by the Mer-People for traveling swiftly through the oceans; its name means "sea-horse." The sea-chariot of Neptune was drawn by Hippocampi.[3] The front part of a Hippocampus was that of a horse with the forelegs ending in powerful webbed fins. Although the rear part of the body had a fish-tail, it also had the long back of a horse with a mane of scalloped fin. Fine scales covered the foreparts, with larger scales elsewhere. Tritons often rode the Hippocampus.

Psychological Attributes: Positive—The ability to quickly assess potential danger in relationships and move away from it. Negative—Viciousness and love of cruelty controlling the emotions.

Magickal Attributes: Call upon the Hippocampus as an astral steed when moving through other planes during meditations dealing with emotional troubles.

Kappa

The Kappa was a demon dwarf entity who lived only in Japanese seas, rivers, or ponds. He resembled a grotesque naked little man or a fur-less, child-sized monkey, with a tortoise shell on his back. The Kappa was yellow-green in color, and sometimes had fish scales or no shell at all. His clawed fingers and toes were webbed and his skin had a green-ish tint. Round eyes peered out over a beaked nose; he also had a pun-gent odor of rotten fish about him. His most distinguishing feature, however, was the circular depression on the crown of his head.

The Kappa liked to lie in wait for people or animals who strayed close to his watery home. Then he leaped from the water, dragged them down to die, and consumed them from the inside out. He had a particular liking for blood; he was also said to rape women.

There were two known methods for escaping the deadly behav-ior of a Kappa. The first was to bow politely when you saw one. The Kappa would bow to you in return, and the water would spill out of the depression on his head. This loss of the water left him powerless until he returned to the water to refill the depression. In the mean-time, the human could escape. The second method was to carve the name of each family member on a cucumber and throw it into the Kappa's water. The Kappa would not attack the people whose names were on the cucumber. However, this cucumber "offering" had to be repeated once a year.

These strange creatures, although very dangerous, have been known to impart certain knowledge to humans, notably about bone-setting. There are also several stories about bargains made with humans and kept by the Kappa.

The gift of the bone-setting talent is told in a story of a Kappa who used to get humans to lock fingers with it, then pull them into the water and kill them. One day a man on horseback played this game with the Kappa, but as soon as their fingers were locked, the man spurred the horse, dragging the Kappa away from the water and spilling the water out of the depression on top of its head. Before he released the Kappa, the creature had to promise to molest no other humans, a promise it kept. In return for its freedom, the Kappa promised to teach the man to set bones; the man and at least one of his descendants in each generation were skilled bone-setters.

Psychological Attributes: One who always wears a mask of friendship, yet seldom has friends because of his or her propensity for double-dealing, lying, and gossiping.

Magickal Attributes: Very dangerous. However, once controlled, it can impart healing information.

KAPPA

The Kraken

The Kraken, a strange creature sometimes confused with the gigantic devil-fish or octopus, was known to the Scandinavian peoples as a dreaded sea menace. It was generally seen in the waters of the North Atlantic and along the coast of Norway. Legend says that there were two Kraken created when the world was made, and these beings will exist as long as the Earth does.

Far larger than a sperm whale, the huge body of this ocean creature was sometimes mistaken for an island. The Kraken was so huge it could easily drag a man from his ship or use its suckered tentacles to crush the ship itself. Whenever a ship was in calm seas, the sailors watched carefully for unusual boiling water, which signaled the Kraken's rise to the surface. There was no escape from its deadly attack once the creature surfaced.

In 1680 C.E. it was reported that a young Kraken became stuck in the narrow channel of Altstahong. When it died, the smell was so horrible that the villagers feared they were in danger of getting some terrible illness from it. In 1752, the Norwegian bishop Pontoppidan personally saw a Kraken and wrote about it. He said that all the sea around the ship for some distance was blackened by the Kraken squirting out its "ink" as a smoke-screen.

The Irish also had tales of sea monsters. The Orc was a sea monster that repeatedly ravaged an island off the coast of Ireland until the creature was slain by a Saracen knight named Rogero.

Psychological Attributes: A person who outwardly appears harmless, but has a dangerous inner and/or malicious personality.

Magickal Attributes: Very dangerous; not recommended.

Liban

This Mermaid is called the "sanctified Mermaid," whose form was accepted by Christians and is seen in carvings in their churches. Liban's story was written by P. W. Joyce in 1894 in his book *Old Celtic Romances*. She is mentioned in *The Annals of the Kingdom of Ireland*, written by the Four Masters; this is an Irish history written in the seventeeth century and which covers the time from creation (as determined by the writers) to the year 1616 C.E. There is one brief account of Liban, attached to the year 558 C.E., when she was caught in a fishing net on Ollarbha strand.

However, Liban's story began several years earlier. Originally, she was a daughter of Eochaid and probably Etain. In the year 90, a sacred spring in Ireland was neglected. It overflowed, forming the huge Lough Neagh. During this flood, Eochaid and his family were drowned, except for Liban and two of his sons. Liban and her pet dog were swept away by the rolling flood water. In answer to her prayers, the girl was changed from the waist down into a salmon, but the upper part of her body remained human. Her dog became an otter.

In the part of the story of her capture in 558 C.E., the fishermen called in the local Christian priest, who supposedly asked Liban if she wanted to "gain a soul" through Christian baptism, or if she wanted to die right then. She "chose" to be baptized, and died immediately afterward.[4]

Psychological Attributes: One who is able to accept and live with the changes life brings.

Magickal Attributes: Accepting harsh changes and turning their influence on life into good.

The Lorelei

This German Mermaid, or Rhine maiden, has become well-known through the works of the composer Richard Wagner. In his opera *Das Rheingold,* three Lorelei, or Mermaids, sing on the rocks of the Rhine River. According to the tale of the *Niebelungen,* the Lorelei owned and guarded a magickal treasure in the Rhine itself.

German legends say that the Lorelei were beautiful young women with fish-tails. Like the Sirens, the Lorelei sang such enchanting songs that they lured unwary boatmen to their doom on the rocks. In fact, a specific rock in the Rhine is named after the Lorelei.

As guardians of magickal treasure in the Rhine, the Lorelei were the keepers of magickal power and spiritual knowledge deep within the subconscious mind.

Although the tales of the Lorelei are primarily German, an English version of this water-maid was called Mary Player. Tradition says that if she swam around a ship three times, she could make it sink.

Psychological Attributes: Positive—A person who has learned to use the power of his or her voice to get people to listen to the truth. Negative—Someone who acts agreeable and helpful so he or she can get something: usually a gift, money, or mention in a will.

Magickal Attributes: Learning magickal secrets; searching for ancient spiritual knowledge.

Melusine

One of the most famous European Mermaids was Melusine. She had a double-tail, which may have been serpentine instead of fish-like; from the navel up, she appeared to be a woman.

Melusine was said to have founded the fortune of the powerful French house of Lusignan. She married Raymond of Poitou and was a good mother and a kind, considerate being. She vanished after her husband criticized her for being half serpent-fish. One of her descendants, Guy de Lusignan, was King of Jerusalem and Cyprus in the twelfth century; the family continued to rule in those countries for three centuries. Before the death of any family member, Melusine would appear on the castle ramparts and cry in a piercing fashion.

The Lusignan family was so famous that several families, including those of Luxembourg and Rohan, had their pedigrees altered to include Melusine in their ancestry. After the Lusignan family died out, Melusine began to give her death-warnings to the French kings. Melusine is mentioned in traditional lore well before the fourteenth century.

Psychological Attributes: One who experiences visions and/or dreams of coming disasters.

Magickal Attributes: Prosperity; warning of disaster or death.

Mermaids and Mermen

Mer-People are known in one form or another around the world. The European Mer-People appear to be distant relatives of the Nereids of the Mediterranean. Their name probably comes from the Indo-European *mori-, mari-* (sea). From this root word came the German *meer* (sea), the Latin *mare* (sea), the English *mere* (lake, sea), and the French *mer* (sea).

In northern Europe, the Mer-People seemed to be found mostly in the colder waters and along the rugged coasts of the Atlantic, although they were seen in other areas as well. Primarily, they ranged from the west coast of Cornwall and along the west coast of the British Isles, all around northern Scotland, and along the rugged cliffs and fjords in Scandinavia and Ireland.

Europeans generally think of the Mermaid only, a human-looking woman down to the hips with a fish's tail. However, there are Mermen, too. The Mermen were usually not as dangerous and tricky as the Mermaids.

The Mer-People primarily live beneath the sea, but sometimes come out onto the rocks in bays and soundings, where they like to sit. Their magnificent underwater palaces sparkle with gold and jewels; a great many of these riches were salvaged from sunken ships. They have their own language but are able to speak the language of the humans along the coasts they frequent. They live on fish and other seafood, but rarely interfere with fishermen unless the humans have offended them. Although folktales tell of Mer-People being captured in the nets of fishermen, this is highly unlikely. These Water-Folk are much too sea-wise and agile for this to happen, unless they have been injured.

The Mer-People care for special herds of certain fish. They also harvest sea vegetation for food.

The Mer-People are human down to the hips; below that they have fish-tails with large flukes, but no dorsal fins. Their upper-body skin is pearly white with a silver sheen. Hair color ranges from a silver blonde to light brown or strawberry blonde; their eyes are either green or blue-green. Although the Mermaids are extremely beautiful and the Mermen very handsome, it is a cold kind of beauty. It is impossible to tell the age of a Mermaid or Merman for the species develops slowly and is immortal. They do not have souls (as humans define the word) and can be vain, jealous, and unforgiving of

MER-PEOPLE

offending humans. They also have supernatural powers, among them the ability to predict the future.

Mermaids can be seen in rivers or shallow seas, singing and combing their long hair. A Mermaid's bewitching voice is said to lure ships onto rocks and men to their deaths. When she is angry, she calls up howling winds and violent storms by dancing through the waves. Several old English ballads tell the story of crews sighting a Mermaid and then their ship being sunk by rocks. The Mermen are muscular, very handsome, and gentle.

Both sexes of the Mer-People have the ability to change their fish-tails into human-like legs so they can go onto dry land and mingle with humans whenever they wish. It is possible that some of the Mer-People spend much of their time, in and out of the water, with legs instead of fish-tails. Although humans and Mer-People seem to have a physical attraction for each other, Mer-People are very different in emotion and character.

Some humans, spying on the shore dancing of a Mer-Person, fell in love and resorted to trickery to marry the creature. These ancient stories are almost always about human males falling in love with Mermaids. It was said that if a human hides the creature's skin, a shell necklace, or some other valuable possession, the Mer-Person must remain on dry land until the object is recovered. In these stories the Mer-Person married the human and even had children. But at some point the being became unhappy, found the hidden object, and returned to the water. Other times, the human only withheld the object until the Mer-Person revealed some secret knowledge or granted the human some supernatural power. The church taught that if the husband could trick the Mermaid into being baptized, she would gain a soul and be unable to return to life in the water.

In a few instances, the husband became disenchanted with his Mermaid wife and her strange ways, sending her back to the sea. These Mermaids either pined away on rocks near the shore or, as in a tale of the Adirondack Indians, returned with other irate water spirits and flooded out the husband and his village.

Mermaids who fell in love with human men always shed their tails and went to live on the land. However, this Mermaid-human man marriage or arrangement rarely worked out. At first the relationship was very passionate, but the Mermaid eventually began to long for the sea. However, there are a few stories of Mermen falling in love with human women. In these tales, the Mermen always turned their lovers into an amphibious form and took them to live deep in the sea.

Children born to a Mer-Person and a human are said to have webbed fingers and/or toes. Excellent swimmers, these offspring were human in appearance and their breathing, but had some of the predictive powers of their sea parent.

Sometimes a human child would make friends with a Mer-Person, particularly a Mermaid. A strong bond would develop, with the Mermaid becoming the child's self-appointed guardian. Any human who mistreated the child would be punished by the guardian Mermaid.

In Scotland there was said to live a branch of the Mer-People who were definitely not friendly toward humans. These were known as the Blue Men of the Muir or the Minch. These beings lived in the strait between Long Island and the Shiant Islands. They threw boulders, wrecked ships, and raised storms in the North Sea. The only way to stop their attack was for the captain of a ship to talk to them in rhyme; it apparently gave the ship time to get away while the Blue Men were unraveling the conversation. Their home was in underwater caves where they were ruled by a chieftain.

To the Germans, the Mermaid was the Lorelei, Meriminni, or Meerfrau; in Iceland, the Marmenill; in Denmark, the Maremind; the Morgans or Morgens in France; and to the Irish, the Merrow. The Matsyanaris of India were portrayed as Nymphs with fish-tails. Chinese sailors believed that Mermaids existed in the China seas. As far back in history as ancient Babylon there was a fish-god who brought the arts of civilization to humans. In Polynesia, the half-human, half-porpoise god Vatea was said to be the father of humans and the gods. Native Americans had a legend of a fish-man with green hair; this strange being was said to have led the Native Americans from a land where they were starving to the North American continent. An African Mermaid named Yemaya had hair made up of long green strands of seaweed; her jewels were shells.

During medieval times, the Siren (previously seen as a bird-woman) took the form of a fish-woman with a huge double tail. Books of alchemy referred to this kind of Siren as the Siren of the Philosophers, or Fish-tailed Aphrodite Marina. Alchemists appear to have thought of her as a cross between a Mermaid and an Irish sheila-na-gig.

In Hispanic folklore there are stories of the Water-Maidens, small human-shaped beings with a star on their forehead. Tradition says their bodies were shimmering and straw-colored, their hair golden. They did not have the webbed fingers of other water sprites, but fingers like those of humans. The Water-Maidens wore white rings on their fingers, and a gold band with black stripes on their left wrists. They sometimes came out of their pools to walk through the meadows. Wherever they stepped, yellow flowers sprang up. Any person fortunate enough to discover these flowers was blessed with happiness. The Water-Maidens had the power to affect and change the way things were or the way events were moving.

From early Assyrian times well into the Persian era, pictures show priests in a fish outfit while practicing healing and exorcism magick. These bearded human-bodied figures have a human face, a fish-head drawn over the top of their heads, and the rest of the fish-body hanging down their backs. It is difficult to determine whether this dress was a handmade costume or the body of an actual fish. There must have been great magickal and spiritual significance for this type of dress, both for priests and the figurines of this type of figure.

In Assyrian, Babylonian, and Mesopotamian art one can see early images of the Mer-People. To the Assyrians, this creature was known as *kulullu* (fish-man) and *kuliltu* (fish-woman). This figure had the typical human upper body and the lower body of a fish. These Mer-People were not only portrayed in sculptures found in palaces and temples, but also used as small figurines in protective magick.

Psychological Attributes: Tolerance; learning how to separate your intellect and animal emotions.

Magickal Attributes: Strong protectors, especially of women. Freedom, imagination, wisdom; predicting storms and future events; finding treasures. The Mer-People can grant wishes and give humans some psychic powers. If you are self-disciplined and dedicated, the Mer-People can enrich your life; if not, the opposite will happen.

Merrow

Many of the German, Scandinavian, and Celtic stories tell of certain kinds of Mer-People who could temporarily lay aside their aquatic skins, take on a human shape, and mingle with humans on shore.

The Merrows, the Irish equivalent of Mermaids, were very beautiful, even though they had fish-tails and webs between their fingers. The females had flowing hair, white gleaming arms, and dark eyes. The males had short arms like flippers, long red noses, green hair and teeth, and small eyes. Both sexes wore red caps which helped them travel through the water; if these caps were stolen, they could not return to the sea. The Merrows were usually friendly, happy creatures.

Although the Irish dreaded seeing the Merrows appear because they heralded the coming of a storm, these sea beings were gentle and often fell in love with humans. The children of such marriages were often covered with tiny scales and had webs between their fingers and toes.

Psychological Attributes: See Mer-People.

Magickal Attributes: Predicting storms; rain.

Nereids

These sea Nymphs of the Mediterranean waters were the fifty grand-daughters of Pontus, the sea god, and Gaea, the Earth Mother. Although in many ways they were similar to Mermaids of other areas of the world, the Nereids did not have fish-tails. They were very beautiful and vain about their appearance.

Most of their time was spent darting through the waves, playing with dolphins. Whenever Poseidon rode out in his ocean chariot surrounded by the Tritons, the Nereids accompanied the sea chariot of his wife, Amphitrite.

Psychological Attributes: One with a happy but slightly irresponsible outlook.

Magickal Attributes: Beauty; happiness; balancing the emotions.

NEREIDS

Nine Daughters of Ran

The Norse goddess Ran was a death deity, the wife of Aegir, god of the sea. She caught in her nets the souls of both those burned at sea in funeral boats and those who drowned.[5]

Ran and Aegir were said to have had nine sea-giantess daughters. Some of the daughters' names were Bylgja (wave), Dufa (diveress), Hefring (the lifting one), Kolga (wave), Gjolp (howler), Greip (grasper), and Udr (wave).

Although Aegir was a jovial deity who brewed ale and hosted dinners for the rest of the gods, his wife and daughters were not so friendly. They liked to cause storms and disasters at sea. While Ran called up a violent storm, the nine daughters would dance wildly on the rising waves until ships were wrecked and sailors drowned. Then Ran with her great net and the daughters with their ghostly white arms would gather these sailors and take them down to Aegir's underwater palace.

In Norse mythology, the god Heimdall was called "the Son of the Nine Waves" because he was born from nine waves through Odhinn's enchantment. This means that the nine daughters of Ran were either his collective mothers or his foster-mothers. This same story is told in the Irish saga of Ruad, son of Rigdonn.

Ruad was on a sea voyage to Norway with three ships when suddenly the ships could no longer move. He dived into the cold waters to find out the reason for this and discovered that three sea-giantesses were hanging onto each ship. These sea-women immediately seized him and carried him down to their underwater palace. They must have been quite beautiful, for Ruad willingly spent a night with each of them, after which they allowed him to return to his ships. As he left, the sea-giantesses told him that one of them would bear him a child. Ruad promised to return to them after his voyage to Norway was completed. After seven years in Norway, however, Ruad headed straight back to Ireland; whether he forgot his promise or had no intention of keeping it, the saga does not say. The sea-giantesses pursued the ships but could not catch up. In anger, they killed the child and threw the head at the father.

Psychological Attributes: One who will get revenge at any cost.

Magickal Attributes: Not recommended except for very experienced magicians; very unpredictable and malicious. Storms, great terror, sailors.

Nixies

The water sprites called Nixies were found in the springs and rivers of Germany; in Iceland they were known as Nickers. In many ways the Germanic Nixies were similar to the Greek Nereids. In Norse the name of their mother was Nott (Mother Night); this goddess was known as Nyx to the Greeks.[6] Both Nott and Nyx were goddesses of chaos energy, and the Nixies and Nereids were their gatherers of human souls for recycling. By the Middle Ages, however, in the minds of humans, the Nixies were similar to the Sirens and other Water-Folk who lured sailors to watery deaths.

The female Nixies liked to sun themselves along the banks just as Mermaids did, but male Nixies were rarely seen by humans. Their physical appearance was humanoid in form, but their skin was lightly scaled. They had greenish skin, green or silver-blonde hair, and silver or bluish silver eyes. The Nixies had no fish-tails; however, their hands and feet were webbed.

Female Nixies were very beautiful. They liked to sit on the banks in the sun, admiring their reflection in the water while they combed their long hair and sang. If they heard a human approaching, they quickly leaped back into the water.

Any handsome young human male who allowed a Nixie to see him was in danger of being lured into the water, for female Nixies were experts at casting love spells through their singing. These young men were seldom seen again, for they were taken deep under the water to the Nixie's lair where they had to stay for at least one year. At the end of this period of enslavement, each human was supposedly free to go, but no one knows what actually happened, since few men thus taken were known to have returned. However, tradition says that any kind of metal would render a Nixie powerless; the creature could even die if exposed to metal for too long.

Nixies never gave up their aquatic forms to join a human on land. If a human crept up on a Nixie and spied on her from the brush, even though he remained unseen, the singing would affect his sanity and common sense; most human men to whom this happened would eventually drown themselves.

Creatures very similar to the Nixies lived in Scandinavia, Estonia, and Latvia. They were called Neckan, Necker, Nakki, or Neck. Superb harpers and singers, these shape-shifting beings were most often seen on the shores of lakes and streams. They tried to entice humans into the water, where they drowned them.

Psychological Attributes: A superficial personality which does not often take responsibility.

Magickal Attributes: Love spells, singing.

Roane

Roane was a Gaelic name for a seal; sometimes these beings were called Seal Maidens. Tradition says that these creatures were a type of Faery who wore seal skins to travel through the seas. However, they could take off the skins and appear in a human shape. The Roane were considered to be the gentlest of all the sea Faeries. They would not even try to get revenge on the seal-catchers who sometimes killed their kin.

Folktales tell of the Roane casting off their seal skins and coming out on the northern shores to dance in the moonlight. In the Scottish Highlands, the Orkneys, and Shetlands, there are many old stories of a mortal fisherman watching these dances, stealing a skin, and thus forcing a Roane (Seal Maiden) to marry him. The marriage was amiable, but as soon as the wife found her seal skin, she escaped back to the sea.

Sometimes the offspring of such a marriage were born with a hereditary horny growth between their fingers. The MacCoddrums of the Seals are the most famous example of this.

Psychological Attributes: See Mermaid.

Magickal Attributes: Music; dance; singing; love.

Rusalki and Vila

The Rusalka (singular) or Rusalki (plural) were water maidens known to the Russian and Slavonic peoples. Their appearance and behavior changed from place to place, and people to people.

The Rusalki were dangerous Russian water sprites, sometimes said to be the souls of drowned women. There seems to be more than one species of Rusalki, especially in Russia, which had one type in the north and another in the southern areas. Both types were extremely dangerous and mischievous whenever humans ventured near water in summer. During the winter months, they lived deep in

RUSALKI

the water, even under ice. But when summer came (at Rusalki Week), the Rusalki had the ability to leave the water and take to the trees in the surrounding forests.

In the gloomy north of Russia, the Rusalki had the appearance of naked drowned women, cadaverous, with eyes that shone with an evil green fire. They liked to lie near or on the water, waiting for careless travelers. They dragged their victims down into the water, where they tortured and bullied the humans before killing them.

The Rusalki of southern Russia were totally different in appearance. They appeared as beautiful young maidens clothed only in gossamer garments, with faces like moonlight. They attracted their victims by singing sweetly to them from the river banks while they wrung out their long hair. When the victim waded into the water to find them, the Rusalki drowned him or her. However, it was said that any man who died this way, died with a smile on his lips.

Along the Rhine and the Danube, this creature was known as a Vila, a gracious and beautiful water being. Those beings of the Dnieper, however, were described as wicked, unattractive girls with uncombed hair. The Rusalki of the Dnieper and Danube sang beautiful songs unknown to their relatives in northern Russia.

The Slavonic cultures said that when the Rusalki left their watery homes during Rusalki Week (the beginning of summer), they did so by climbing up the slim branches of willow or birch which hung over the water. At night, when moonlight filled the forest, they swung on the branches and called out to each other; then they slipped down the trees and danced in the clearings. They sometimes even went into the farmers' fields to dance. The southern Slavs said that the Rusalki's dancing areas could be found by looking for places where the grass grew thicker and the wheat more abundant.

Besides drowning travelers, the Rusalki had other bad habits. They could ruin the harvest with torrential rain, tear up fishing nets, destroy dams and water mills, or even steal clothes, linen, and thread from human women.

However, these Russian water spirits feared one herb. Travelers could protect themselves from the Rusalki when they journeyed near water by carrying a few leaves of wormwood *(Artemisia absinthium)*. Wormwood sprinkled on anything a Rusalki might steal or destroy would also keep them away. If the Rusalki were particularly troublesome in a region, large quantities of wormwood would be sprinkled over the river or pond.

The Vilas were also known in Dalmatia. In that culture, these water sprites were called Rugulja, "Horned Ones."

Psychological Attributes: One with a chameleon-like personality.

Magickal Attributes: Very dangerous. Abundance and good crops.

Scylla and Charybdis

In Greek mythology there were two strange Water-Folk who began life as humans; these were Scylla and Charybdis.

Scylla was first a beautiful water sprite. Myths vary on whether she was the daughter of Phorcys and Crataeis, Typhon and Echidna, or of Poseidon.

A fisherman named Glaucus fell in love with her. However, Scylla did not return his love, but scorned his pleas. In desperation, Glaucus went to the enchantress Circe and tried to get her to cast a love spell on the water sprite. Circe refused, telling Glaucus to forget his love for Scylla because it would never work. Glaucus was very angry and refused Circe's advice.

Instead of punishing Glaucus, however, Circe decided to punish the innocent water sprite. The enchantress brewed a mixture of poisonous herbs and threw this into the sea where Scylla lived. When Scylla swam out for her daily exercise, she suddenly found herself turning into a terrifying monster, rooted to that place along the cliffs. Myth says Scylla then had twelve legs and six huge dogs' heads on long snake-like necks. The heads yelped like dogs, but it was her bite that was deadly, for Scylla lived on fish, dolphins, and any sailors she can get. Scylla took up residence in a lair in the sea cliffs on the Italian side of the strait.

Another version of this story[7] says Scylla was seduced by her father, Poseidon. When Amphitrite, Poseidon's wife, found out, she went to Circe and asked her to punish Scylla, which the sorceress did with the magick potion.

Today, Scylla is the name of a great rock which juts out of the sea at the tip of Italy, in the strait between Italy and Sicily.

Charybdis is still said to live under a rock on the Sicilian side. She trapped sailors and ships by creating a gigantic whirlpool. The

SCYLLA

sucking in and blowing out three times a day by Charybdis can still be seen in this strait.

Psychological Attributes: One who either strongly dislikes their own or the opposite sex.

Magickal Attributes: Extremely dangerous; not recommended.

Selkies

Among the various types of British Mermaids are the Seal-Folk of the Faroe Islands; every ninth night these creatures were said to shed their skins and, in human form, dance on the beaches.

The people of the Shetland Islands say that the Selkies who lived in their waters only wore their seal skins to get from one place to another, that their true shape was a human-like form. However, unlike the gentler Roane, the Selkies would exact revenge against seal-hunters by raising storms and sinking the seal-boats.

Tales from the Orkney Islands also say that the Selkies' natural form was a human, air-breathing shape. They say that the seal-people lived in underwater worlds enclosed in great air bubbles, only wearing the skins to get from one region of air to another.

The Selkies were thought to be more beautiful than humans, with large liquid eyes. Although female Selkies would only stay with a human man if he stole her skin, and then only until she recovered it, male Selkies often came ashore to court mortal women. Amorous creatures, these sea-males might have a relationship, but they never remained long with a human lover. In the ballad "The Great Selkie of Sule Skerry," a male Selkie had a child with a human woman; although he at first left them, he came back later because he knew the woman's husband would kill both her and the child.

The offspring of a human and Selkie union were said to have webs between their fingers and toes. Often this characteristic became a hereditary feature in a family. In the Shetland Islands and Iceland, tradition says that if a human woman wished to have a child by a Selkie she must weep seven tears into the sea at night.

Psychological Attributes: See Mermaid.

Magickal Attributes: Raising storms, especially over water.

Tarroo-Ushtey

This strange creature was a water-bull from the Isle of Man. The Tarroo-Ushtey [tar-oo ushtar] was less dangerous than the Cabyll-Ushtey and the Each Uisge, but it was best to have no contact with it. This bull-formed creature was believed to have round ears and glittering eyes. It lived primarily in the sea but came out on land to graze along with the cattle of humans. However, the Tarroo-Ushtey could never be captured or tamed.

Psychological Attributes: A person who lives life as he or she sees fit, not influenced by current trends.

Magickal Attributes: Less dangerous than any of the other water-bulls, but still must be handled with great care. Use as a guide when venturing into the astral kingdoms of the Water-Folk.

Tritons

The Tritons were Mermen of the Mediterranean. In some ways they resembled the Mermen of other waters, but were less attractive to humans in their appearance and manners. Tritons had a forked fish-tail, but a human torso from the hips upward. However, they also had sharp fish teeth and webbed fingers with long claws. Their chests and bellies had scales and fins. These scales were silvery, fading to silvery-blue on their legs when they assumed a form which allowed them to go onto land. Their hair was usually deep blue or blue-green.

Like other Mer-People, the Tritons had the ability to change their fish-tails into legs and go onto the land. Whenever they did this, though, they retained the webs between their fingers and toes and their sharp teeth. These creatures were renowned for playing malicious tricks on seamen.

Unlike the northern Mermen, the Tritons did not fall in love with human females. They were, however, lustful creatures who thought nothing of raping any female who came near them. They liked to go ashore in seaside towns to get disgustingly drunk and vandalize everything in sight. Humans often had to form posses to deal violently with gangs of Tritons, the only deterrent these creatures understood.

At Tanagra there is a legend about a Triton who caused great trouble by coming ashore each night, desolating the countryside, and ravaging women. In desperation, the people found a jar of the strongest wine and put it on the beach. When the Triton passed out from drinking the wine, a fisherman cut off his head. To commemorate the event and discourage any other troublesome Tritons, the people put up the statue of a headless Triton in the local temple of Dionysus.

The only occupation these sea entities had was to harness the dolphins to their grandfather Poseidon's chariot and swim before him when he journeyed across the oceans. Blowing their conch shell horns, the Tritons gave warning for all to stay out of Poseidon's way.

The father of the Tritons was the sea deity Triton, a peaceful and helpful entity. His name was used to describe the whole race of Mediterranean Mermen. Triton, who was the son of Poseidon, had the lower part of a dolphin and the upper part of a human man. His favorite section of the coastline was Libya. This entity often emerged

TRITON

from his deep sea palaces to aid seafarers who found themselves in trouble. Using his conch shell trumpet, Triton could calm the roughest seas or create a storm. He also had prophetic ability. His chariot was drawn by sea-horses with crayfish-claw hooves.

Psychological Attributes: One who prefers short-term, unemotionally involved sexual relationships. A person to whom satisfaction of his or her own desires and needs always comes first.

Magickal Attributes: The Tritons—Malicious, drunken, and very dangerous. The deity Triton—Prophecy; safety while on water; calming a storm.

Vodyanoi

Throughout Russia there are legends of many water monsters, a great many of whom live in mill ponds. These creatures were called Vodyanoi, a general term that covered several species. However, they all had one common characteristic: the Vodyanoi lived an entire life during each monthly Moon cycle. They appeared to grow older as the Moon got older, and became young again with the New Moon.

The Vodyanoi had several different physical appearances, which points to the possibility of several different species of them. Some of them looked like old men with green hair and beards; the hair and beard colors gradually changed to white with the waning Moon. Sometimes they appeared as naked beautiful women with green hair; their hair changed to white and they became old and wrinkled as the Moon aged. Other times the Vodyanoi took the form of a gigantic fish, covered with moss and waterweed, or a snarling, vicious monster with huge fiery eyes. One could never be certain about floating logs in Vodyanoi territory, for such a log was often one of these creatures in a shape-shifted form.

Vodyanoi were not generally benign entities. Like many malicious water spirits, they often grabbed people from the banks of ponds and tried to drown them. They had a special hatred for watermills because they obstructed the flow of water. Mill owners took care not to offend any of the Vodyanoi deliberately, for if this happened, the creatures would try to destroy them by causing a drought or flood. People knew of the presence of Vodyanoi by their excessive splashing and their audible growls and low-voiced complaints heard from the mill pond.

Psychological Attributes: One with a short temper who sees problems everywhere, even when there are none.

Magickal Attributes: Very malicious; can cause drought or flood.

ENDNOTES

1. *Fairy Tales from the Isle of Man.* In this book, Sophia Morrison tells of the traditional family relationship between the Sayle family and a local Mermaid.
2. For an example of a magician with a separable soul, read the story of the Firebird. (See Chapter 8.)
3. Manly P. Hall. *The Secret Teachings of All Ages.*
4. Supposedly Liban died from the baptism, but if Christian policy was followed, she was probably killed as were other "sinners" who accepted the Christian religion, thinking they would then be free to return to their natural home. Nowhere does it say that anyone gave Liban the third choice of returning to the sea.
5. H. R. Ellis Davidson. *Gods & Myths of the Viking Age.*
6. Brian Branston. *Gods of the North.*
7. Robert Graves. *The White Goddess.*

17

Creatures of
the Stony Stare

The Gorgons are familiar magickal creatures from Greek myth who had the ability to turn humans to stone by their stare. The idea behind the "evil eye" probably originated with these mythical creatures who could kill or turn to stone anyone who fell under their gaze. We still subconsciously recall the powers of the Gorgons, the Basilisk, and Cockatrice when we speak of people having "a stony stare," "a heart of stone," or "a stone face."

These creatures of the stony stare symbolize unhealthy solidification in human life. When you allow yourself to be locked into a routine, whether it be in habits, daily living, spiritual ideas, or the general way you look at things, you are allowing aspects of these creatures to dominate your life.

Basilisk and Cockatrice

The Basilisk and Cockatrice became known as the same creature by the Middle Ages. Earlier, however, they were two separate, but vaguely similar, fabulous beasts. A silver sculpture from about 1600 shows a Basilisk with a lizard-like head, webbed and clawed front feet, two wings, and a serpent-like tail. A picture of a Cockatrice from about the same time portrays the creature with a cock's body, two wings, a spiked head, and a serpent's tail.

The Basilisk was a reptile, while the Cockatrice was a combination of rooster and snake with wings. Both creatures were said to have the ability to turn to stone anything they saw. Their breath was considered to be venomous, as was the touch of their bodies and blood. This poison was said to travel through any weapon used to kill the Basilisk or Cockatrice, thus killing the person holding the weapon.

However, Aristotle believed that if the Basilisk saw its reflection in a mirror it would turn to stone. The person holding the mirror, of course, had to avoid looking at the creature.[1] Another legendary method of killing either of these creatures was to carry a weasel or mongoose with you. These animals would supposedly attack and kill the Basilisk or Cockatrice on sight and were immune to the deadly stare.

If wounded, the animal could heal itself by eating rue *(Ruta graveolens* or "herb of grace"), the only plant able to withstand the fatal stare or breath of the Basilisk or Cockatrice.

The Basilisk was the older of the two creatures. It lived in warmer climates, and was usually found in deserts. It was yellow in color with glittering toad-like eyes, pointed wings, and a tail curled up over its back like the stinger of a scorpion. It was not a large creature; the ancients described it as being less than two feet long. Its head had three bony or horny protuberances which resembled a crown. Some writers even said it had a three-pointed tail.[2] A few ancient writers believed that the Basilisk originated from the serpents that writhed on Medusa's head.[3]

Basilisk comes from a Greek word *(basiliskos)* meaning "little king," or King of Small Serpents. In Latin it was called *regulus,* which has the same meaning. Pliny wrote that the Basilisk was the king of the smaller reptiles; its hissing was said to drive away snakes. He said that this creature could split rocks, walked in a fairly upright position, and propelled its body over the ground with legs, not by crawling as snakes do. Ancient writers said it could split rocks with its breath and lived in wastelands where it kept and guarded treasure. Presumably, this wasteland was created by its deadly breath.

The Basilisk appears to have been known primarily to Europeans, although there is some mention of them in the East. At one time there was a similar creature which was said to live in Iceland. This creature was known as a Skoffin; its appearance and behavior was similar to that of the Basilisk. The only thing that could kill a Skoffin was the stare of another Skoffin.

Today, the name Basilisk has been given to a harmless member of the iguana family.

The Cockatrice appears to be an entirely different creature from the Basilisk. The word Cockatrice comes from the Greek *ikhneumon* (track); this word gave birth to the medieval Latin *calcatrix* (tracker, hunter) and the Old French *cocatris* (Cockatrice). Medieval writers got carried away when describing the origin of the Cockatrice. The Cockatrice was said to have been hatched from the yolkless egg of a male nine-year-old chicken during the days of the Dog Star. Legend says that the cock laid the egg in a dung heap where it was hatched by a toad or snake.

There is evidence that bodies of old roosters sometimes contain a small egg-shaped globe, which is the result of putrefaction. This may be the basis for the strange legend of the birth of the Cockatrice.

BASILISK AND COCKATRICE

The Cockatrice appears to have been accepted more by the Western Christian populations than by Pagans. The records of its appearance were all recorded by Christians, such as the tale of the Cockatrice which supposedly appeared in Rome during the time of Pope Leo X; the creature was blamed for a virulent plague. In 1202 C.E. a Cockatrice was said to have been dragged out of a well in Vienna. In 1598 another, in the cellar of an abandoned house in Warsaw, was blamed for the death of two little girls; it was supposedly killed by a man wearing a suit of mirrors sewn onto leather.

Psychological Attributes: A person with a venomous and hard-hearted attitude toward anyone who disagrees with him or her or of whom he or she is jealous. One who is constantly wishing bad things to happen to people he or she doesn't like.

Magickal Attributes: Discovering the treasure within yourself; developing talents; uncovering hidden spiritual secrets.

Gorgons

The Gorgons, especially Medusa, are well-known from Greek mythology. There was disagreement on the number of Gorgons, though the usual number was listed as three. There was also disagreement as to whether the Gorgons were creatures of the Underworld, the Earth, or the Air.

The most commonly known of this trio, daughters of an ancient sea god, was Medusa (Cunning One or Queen), who could turn people to stone by her stare or glance. Only Medusa had ever been totally human. At one time she had been a beautiful priestess of Athene who profaned the temple by copulating with Poseidon in it. As punishment, Athene changed Medusa into a hideous and deadly monster. Her body became covered with scales like a snake; her hair turned into writhing serpents; her teeth became fangs; and her gaze turned humans to stone. She was slain by Perseus; he gave Medusa's head to Athene, who mounted it on her shield. This head (Gorgoneum) had a protruding tongue, snake hair, and huge fangs.

The other two sisters, Stheno (Mighty One) and Euryale (Wandering One or Far-springer), always appeared in their hideous, non-human forms. They also had claws of brass, wings, and protruding tongues from which dripped poisonous saliva. The Gorgons were

GORGON

related to the Graiae, three old women who had the ability to see into the future but were dangerous to humans. Not only could the Gorgons turn any human to stone by their stare, their snake-hair could inflict a venomous bite.

Psychological Attributes: One who has to live through conditions beyond the endurance of the conscious mind, yet manages to survive and revive his or her life.

Magickal Attributes: Revenge, retribution, protection. Setting up a reflective protection to return dark magick.

ENDNOTES

1. Walter Beltz. *God & The Gods.*
2. Gertrude and James Jobes. *Outer Space.*
3. Herbert Silberer. *Hidden Symbolism of Alchemy & the Occult Arts.*

18

Gargoyles

L ong before the Disney cartoon *Gargoyles* made
its appearance on videotape and television,
Gargoyles held a special fascination for me. I
never thought of them as the "bogie under the bed"
type of creature, but as powerful, Otherworld
beings I wanted very much to know firsthand. A
great many people shudder when they see Gargoyle
statues, thinking of them as ugly, repulsive creations
better left on high roofs where they are seldom seen
except by the very curious. However, small Gargoyle
statues are becoming popular as decorations either
inside or outside private homes.

Gargoyle decorations on buildings are commonly associated with such cities as Paris and Old
World places, but they also exist in several American
cities, such as New York and the Minneapolis-St.
Paul area. Among the true Gargoyles are represen-
tations of the Old Gods, mythical creatures, and

even ordinary animals. The carvings of the Old Gods, mythical beings, and animals should not be termed "Gargoyles," for the true Gargoyle is a totally different and easily recognized being.

The creatures we call Gargoyles first made a widespread appearance in European Gothic art and, during those times, symbolized negative[1] cosmic forces. It may well be that the idea of carved Gargoyles came from the superconscious mind of the Old Norse-Germanic cultures, for these people understood that the frightening and hideous did not necessarily mean "evil" or "demonic." In a short time the Gothic European Gargoyle came to be classified with the Mediterranean Grotesques, which were a much older depiction of the same type of being.

When the Gothic cathedrals were built, their roofs were almost covered with Gargoyle sculptures. The medieval builders were following an ancient belief that sacred or holy places could be protected by surrounding them, or at least having present on the buildings, ugly, threatening guardian-sculptures to keep any truly evil influences at bay.

Orthodox religion, however, immediately explained away the presence of Pagan Gargoyles as symbols of the demons of the Christian hell. In Christian architecture, Gargoyles were never allowed to occupy the center of the building or design, the place reserved for angels; they were relegated to the edges in keeping with their Christian-appointed position as slaves and minions of the devil.[2]

Grotesques, which is actually another name for Gargoyle-like creatures, can be traced far back in history to the ancient cultures in the Middle East. They were favored and widely used by the ancient Romans and became popular again from the fifteenth century C.E. onward. Grotesque means "a creature from the grotto." This refers to the pre-Christian European worship of certain deities or Nature spirits in grottoes and caves.

As evidence of pre-Christian knowledge of Gargoyles, there exists a small statue, known as the man-eating monster of Noves, in Bouches-du-Rhone, France; it dates from the third century B.C.E. The features of this creature match no living animal. Protruding from its jaws is a human arm with a bracelet on it. Its front paws grasp two human heads.

Gargoyles and Grotesques are basically the same, although architects use these terms to mean two separate types of building decoration. Gargoyles are commonly thought of as only architectural rain spouts for buildings. During the Gothic period these stone carriers of rain were carved in the forms of grotesque monsters and "demons."

The Grotesques were used for decoration and had no additional function. They were portrayals of ancient deities, fabulous animals, and animal-like forms peering out of foliage. Another meaning of the word Grotesque is "grotto-like," probably coming from the Italian *pittura grottesco* (wall paintings in an underground place). Grottesco has come to mean "fanciful, fantastic." Grotto and crypt are basically the same word, the source of which is the Greek *krupte* (hidden place). Therefore, Gargoyles and Grotesques are, underneath all the hair-splitting, the same kinds of creatures: fantastic-looking, often hideous beings who guard sacred places.

The word Gargoyle is apparently taken from the Greek *gargarizein* (gargle) and the Latin *gargarizare* (gargle) or *gurgulio* (gullet, windpipe, or trachea). Most people take the "gargle" meaning as referring to the expulsion of water, but there is another, more appropriate, hidden symbolism in the word Gargoyle. The trachea or gullet not only expels things, but also takes in air. Magicians and mystics have always said that ordinary air is filled with spiritual power, a benefit to those who understand how to tap and use it. This is a clue to the real purpose of Gargoyles.

Some of the oldest examples of Gargoyles erected under Christian influence are in Europe. The Cathedral of Notre Dame in Paris has many, as does the Cathedral at Freiburg, Germany. These sculptures have a great variety of forms. They can have horns, wings, clawed feet, beaked heads, goat's beards, and even women's breasts on occasion. Some of the feet are webbed and/or are fish-fins. Others have scales or feather-like overlays on their necks. Bat-like faces with wrinkled snouts, muzzles with semi-flattened noses, every kind of Grotesque face imaginable can be seen on Gargoyles.

However, all Gargoyles are not frightening creatures. Reproductions of one little Gargoyle found on the roof of the Notre Dame Cathedral in Paris are now becoming popular. This Gargoyle is quite human-like and sits with his knees bent, his arms around them, and his big toes crossed. The story behind this small creature says that when the Cathedral was being built,[3] Marie Therese (a nun from a convent in Provence) was not happy with the types of Gargoyles being put on the roof. She disguised herself as a man, went to the work-site in Paris, and carved little Dedo [dee-doe], as she called him. Then she put him on a ledge on a high roof. For centuries, no

DEDO

one was aware of Dedo's existence, until a small boy fell off a roof-ledge and rolled up against him. The French lovingly call Dedo the "petite gargouille."

Many European and American cities still have Gargoyles on the roofs of a great many of their buildings. Most people are not aware of these creatures perched high above the streets. However, the Gargoyles are very much aware of humans. They may sit on their perches, moving only at night or during heavy rainstorms, but they have a definite life-energy. As Stephen King[4] suggests, we might not see them, but they see us all the time. Even when we don't see them, they are watching us. They are alive in their own way.

Most people have been so brainwashed by Christianity and its teachings about grotesque-looking creatures being demons that we have an inbred fear of Gargoyles, without really knowing anything about them. Even the faces of those Gargoyles who look halfway benign are alien to us. They are faces which might well haunt the dark and our dreams.

Gargoyles can be roughly divided into several categories, some of which overlap others. There are "spitting" Gargoyles, the ones whose tongues are protruding; those whose mouths are open in a little pucker can fall into this category, for they look as if they could spit or blow water on you at any moment. "Gnawing" Gargoyles tend to have something in their mouths, sometimes a human arm, sometimes a whole human body. Many Gargoyles are "hunkered," meaning they are sitting with their knees drawn up and their arms or paws around their knees. There are several examples of "cross-toed" Gargoyles besides little Dedo. Many Gargoyles have wings, most raised, some folded. "Horned" Gargoyles may have one or two horns on their heads. "Perching" Gargoyles look as if they are ready to leap into the air.

Gargoyles were slow to emigrate to the Western Hemisphere, perhaps because they were waiting for people of this Western culture to believe in them. Knowing how to contact and work with Gargoyles is a slow process for any human, as the ancient knowledge of Gargoyle magick was entirely destroyed.

Gargoyles, although now commonly seen perched on the roofs of buildings, originally preferred to live among ancient ruins or in underground caves when they appeared in the physical. Later, they began to inhabit tall structures, such as castles and cathedrals. Those with wings do not constantly flap them, as birds do; rather they move from one place to another with gliding motions and only a rare movement of the wings. Since all Gargoyles are experts in telekinesis and the ability to move effortlessly through time and space, they can appear and disappear in the blink of an eye.

The marine-type Gargoyles dwell in shallow water, with their lairs in undersea caverns; they can use their wings to "swim" with the water currents. They particularly like to perch on sea cliffs under the

NOTRE DAME GARGOYLES

Full Moon; they blend so well with the shadows that it is rare for a human to see them at all.

The Gargoyle's voice makes a gargling or gurgling sound when it communicates telepathically and/or verbally. The voice may sound "gravelly" or as if it comes from a very deep well or cavern.

Gargoyles can be ferocious if approached in the wrong manner and with the wrong intentions, for example, if a magician tries to send them to kill someone. This is not to say that Gargoyles cannot be sent to bring evil-doers to justice, for they can. However, if the cause is not just, Gargoyles can become unreliable tricksters who bring your negative desires back home to you. Because of their magickal nature, Gargoyles are instantly able to determine a magician's true motives for contacting them. Gargoyles are often the guardians of dimensional doorways into other Worlds beyond the physical.

MARINE GARGOYLE

Gargoyles help drain away the thoughts, events, and people which cause rot and erosion on all levels of our lives. They create a catharsis in our lives, freeing us for better things. Their power is undeniable.

Some Pagans are learning to use a Gargoyle statue as a physical receptacle for the normal, but disturbing and unhealthy, negative thoughts they have. This is not done in order to build up a reservoir of negative power to use in an "evil" way, but to safely rid one's self of negativity. Gargoyles soak up this negative energy, then transform it into an energy pattern which they can use. Of course, Gargoyles do not live in statues. The statues are simply a symbol of these creatures, a touch-point between you and the Gargoyles on the astral plane.

Sometimes a magician has to fight fire with fire, not necessarily because of another magician, but most often because of the followers of other religions. When you find yourself in such a situation, fighting for your own life and the life of your family, your well-being, and the right to worship freely as you choose, turn to the Gargoyles. Angry Gargoyles always remind me of the sign with a picture of Rotweilers which says: "We can make it to the fence in three seconds. Can you?" Like Dragons, Gargoyles make excellent personal and residential guardians.

Gargoyles are a symbol of the world of psychic phenomena and of the coherent unfolding of existence and events. They can help you discover your purpose in this life and how you fit into the cosmic events happening at any given moment; nearly all humans are not in their present life for some earth-shattering purpose, but simply to learn and grow, to correct mistakes, and to better themselves. Humans find it more difficult to discover this "mundane" purpose than to identify one of great importance.

Working with Gargoyles can help you discover and understand lost knowledge and how to apply it in a practical way to your everyday life. They are superb, no-nonsense teachers of ancient spiritual mysteries and disciplines. However, never try to trick, manipulate, or coerce Gargoyles into doing something for you that they do not want to do. Irritated and angry Gargoyles always manage to punish you for such behavior before they disappear from your life, leaving you to stew in the troubles you have created.

Psychological Attributes: Positive—One who pursues spiritual goals while keeping his or her activities out of the public eye. Negative—A person who uses "spiritual" knowledge to control others through fear.

Magickal Attributes: Protection; guarding the land, home, occupants, and possessions. Companionship and protection while on astral journeys or during meditations and rituals. Removing negative events or people from your life. Developing the psychic. Researching past lives in order to understand your present life. Discovering your true purpose in this life. Reconnecting with ancient knowledge and teachings.

ENDNOTES

1. Negative does not mean evil. This type of energy is merely part of the circle of power which makes up the universe. It is a necessary balance to positive power, just as the Crone aspect of the Goddess is a necessary power of the Triple Goddess.

2. J. E. Cirlot. *A Dictionary of Symbols.*

3. The Cathedral of Notre Dame was built in the twelfth century C.E. In 1845, Eugene Emmanuel Viollet-le-Duc was given the task of restoring the building to its original Gothic splendor. He designed many of its present-day Gargoyles.

4. Stephen King. *Nightmares in the Sky.*

19

Other Magickal, Mythical Creatures

There are so many wonderful magickal beings and creatures who did not fall into one of the previous categories that I had to set aside this chapter for them.

The elemental beings connected with the Elements of Earth, Air, Fire, and Water have been known and acknowledged for centuries by philosophers, initiates, and magicians. The ancient Mystery Religions and schools of magick taught their pupils how to communicate with these beings and gain their cooperation in important undertakings. The only stern warnings were given about contacting the Fire elementals (see Salamanders, listed later in this chapter).

Initiates were told not to betray the trust of any elementals or deceive them, for to do so would eventually bring sorrow and possible destruction down upon the offender. The mystics said that to use the power of the elementals to gain temporary power over others would cause these elemental beings to turn against the magician.

Elemental beings regularly meet at certain times of the year in great numbers, rejoicing in the beauty and harmony of Nature. Shakespeare describes one such meeting in *A Midsummer Night's Dream*. Summer Solstice (Midsummer) is still believed to be an extremely active time for Faeries, Elves, Gnomes, and all the other elemental beings.

When the Christians gained control, they did not dispute the existence of these elemental beings known to the Pagans. They simply classified every elemental creature and being under the title of demon, which means something which is evil, and said they all worked for the Christian devil.

Barbegazi

In the high mountainous areas of France and Switzerland live the Gnome-like creatures called the Barbegazi. The name might come from a Swiss word which means "frozen beards." Unlike many other Nature spirits, the Barbegazi hibernate during the summer months, coming out only after the first heavy snowfalls of winter. It is rare to see them when the temperature is above zero. They are seldom found below the tree-line. A few Barbegazi have been trapped by mountaineers and taken to alpine villages; these Barbegazi seldom lived more than a few hours.

Barbegazi look much like Gnomes from other areas of

BARBEGAZI

the world except for their very large feet and their hair and beards, which look like icicles. Their large feet enable these creatures to get about the snowy regions as if they wore skis or snowshoes. The Barbegazi can run swiftly over the snow or "ski" down almost vertical slopes. These large feet are also useful for digging; they can conceal themselves in seconds, or dig themselves out of avalanches with no trouble. They like to ride avalanches down the mountains.

It is nearly impossible to tell the females from the males, except at close range. Both male and female Barbegazi wear white fur garments which help them blend into the snowy scenery. Their normal communication sounds like the whistle of marmots, a small mammal native to the Swiss Alps. However, for long-distance communication, the Barbegazi make an eerie hooting which can be mistaken for the wind or an Alpine horn.

The homes of these Gnome-like beings are close to the summits of the high peaks. They excavate a network of caves and tunnels which can be entered only through tiny openings. These openings to the outer world are hidden by curtains of icicles. The Barbegazi usually appear only when blizzards and freezing temperatures have forced the mountaineers from the higher altitudes. There is little actually known about the lifestyle of the Barbegazi.

Their attitude toward humans is generally friendly, although they tend to avoid them as much as possible. Some humans living in the region say that the Barbegazi are very helpful, but the credit is more often than not given to the St. Bernard dogs. Others believe that these little creatures will warn of coming avalanches by whistling or hooting.

Psychological Attributes: One who willingly helps others and demands no recognition of that help.

Magickal Attributes: Very helpful in warning of coming winter storms; rescue from dangerous situations.

Bogies

The term Bogie covers a wide range of mischievous beings and creatures who like to live in darkness or semi-darkness. They are also called Bogey-men, Bogles, Bog-a-boos, Boggies, and Bogey-beasts. On the Isle of Man they are known as Boggans. They are usually fairly harmless to humans.

These little troublesome beings are rather vague in appearance with hollow, gleaming eyes. Their wispy form is often mistaken for a puff of dust.

Bogies make their homes in deep cupboards, cellars, barns, lofts, hollow trees, abandoned mines, caves, crevices, under sinks, and other similar places. They particularly like cluttered storage places. Although people think Bogies merely frequent old houses, they have been known to get into modern homes as well. However, homes and old barns are not the only places infested with Bogies. They have been known to take up residence in junk shops, tool sheds, second-hand stores, cluttered law offices, and even school buildings.

Although one may occasionally hear a restless Bogie making muffled creaks and thumps, Bogies only come out of their hiding places at night or when everything is very quiet. They delight in creating minor mischief such as hiding things, messing up stacks of work papers, or pulling the covers off sleeping humans. One of their favorite tricks is to hover behind people and make them uneasy. In some ways, Bogies are much like Goblins and Gremlins, but have less imagination.

In Ireland, a similar species of beings are known as Ballybogs. They are very small, quite ugly, with long, thin arms and legs. They are not as intelligent as the English Bogies.

Psychological Attributes: A person who delights and revels in causing trouble for others.

Magickal Attributes: Never invite Bogies into your home or even your ritual circle! They are notoriously difficult to get rid of.

Bokwus

This solitary creature is part of Northwestern Native American mythology. Bokwus is rarely seen, but can be felt whenever one enters thick, dimly-lit forests of northwest America. His evil face, painted in bright war paint, might be glimpsed as he peers around tree trunks. His rustling in the brush can be heard following any hunter, hiker, or fisherman.

Bokwus is most dangerous, however, around the rushing water of rivers. He waits until fishermen are absorbed in their pursuit, then sneaks silently upon them while they stand on a slippery rock and pushes them into the river. As soon as the fisherman drowns, Bokwus grabs the soul and takes it back to his forest home.

Psychological Attributes: One who loves to stalk or spy on others.

Magickal Attributes: Very dangerous; not recommended.

Brownies

Scotland is the original home of authentic Brownies. When the Scottish people began emigrating to other parts of the world, Brownies went with them. Now Brownies can be found in a great many countries. However, there are similar indigenous beings in other countries. In North Africa they are known as Yumboes and in China as Choa Phum Phi.

Brownies are small beings about three feet tall, usually male, with rather flat faces and lots of hair on their bodies. The typical Scottish Brownie has black eyes, slightly pointed ears, and long, agile fingers. Brownies ordinarily wear little brown suits, cloaks, and caps, although on occasion one will be seen wearing green clothes.

Brownies prefer to be out and about during the night, but some of them will appear during daylight. If they have not attached themselves to a household, they will take up residence in old hollow trees or ruins.

They are cheerful and helpful, unless offended, preferring to live in harmony with humans. They dislike cheating and lying, messy people, and ministers. Their smiles and happy dispositions particularly attract the attention of small children who find it easy to see and communicate with brownies. Children are fascinated by Brownie stories and

HIGHLAND BROWNIE

games, such as making daisy chains. Some Brownies will attach themselves to a family and stay with them for generations.

However, Brownies are just as eager to help human adults. In times when nearly every household had a cow and chickens, the Brownies would help with the milking and get the hens into the coop at night. Nowadays, Brownies have found other little tasks to do, but they are not overly fond of any kind of machinery. Today you might spot a Brownie entertaining a baby to keep it from crying, giving you subtle warnings that a pet or your child is ill or in danger, tending to house plants, or singing to you in his gruff little voice while you work on a hobby.

Tradition says that to give a Brownie a gift or thank him will make him leave. However, if the gift or thanks is given with tact and in secret, Brownies are not offended.

Welsh Brownies are called Bwbachod [boobachod]. They distinctly do not like teetotalers or minsters. A Manx cousin of the Brownie is known as the Fenoderee [fin-ord-er-ree]; however, he is large, very hairy, and ugly.

If you have Brownies in your home, appreciate them but do not be open or profuse with gifts or praise, for they may take this as an insult. Brownies inhabiting any place will protect against an invasion of Goblins and many other malicious little beings.

Psychological Attributes: One who enjoys working with his or her hands in areas such as gardening, farming, crafts, etc.

Magickal Attributes: Getting rid of other troublesome elemental creatures. Seeking friendships; looking for a new home.

Domovoy

Russian and Slavic tradition say that certain little household spirits have lived in the homes of humans from the beginning. The Domovoy (singular, and usually the title for the male) is rarely seen, and his wife (the Domovikha) is never seen. Seeing these beings is considered to be extremely unlucky, while hearing the Domovoy can be either fortunate or unfortunate. When the Domovoy is seen, he can easily be mistaken for a dog or cat; however, he is a very small man covered with silky hair.

The Domovoy and Domovikha are thought to be benign creatures. The Domovoy lives under the stove or doorstep, while his wife lives in the cellar. When a family moves into a new home, it is considered a good idea to put a piece of bread under the stove to attract the Domovoy and Domovikha. They are considered extremely loyal to the family they adopt, often doing favors for them.

The Domovoy never speaks to humans, but if he chatters and murmurs softly to himself at night, it is thought that everything in the family's life will be pleasant. If he moans, however, the family knows that misfortune is coming. When the Domovoy weeps, it is a sure sign that someone in the family will soon die.

Psychological Attributes: One whose emotions and sympathies are easily aroused. A person whose life revolves around his or her home.

Magickal Attributes: Tarot or rune-readings into the future. Prediction of all kinds.

Dwarfs

Dwarfs originally lived in Scandinavian and Germanic countries, but like many other little creatures, emigrated to other countries. Although the Dwarfs are sometimes confused with Gnomes by uninformed humans, there is a vast difference in appearance. The Dwarfs are small beings with large heads and gnarled faces. Their skin coloring, hair, and eyes tend to be Earth colors.

The Dwarfs are associated with the North, the position of earthly gain and powers. The name of their king is given as Gob or Ghom, showing a possible relationship to the word Goblin.

Humans seldom see Dwarfs because they live underground, only coming to the surface for certain festivities. Dwarf cities are sometimes in vast caves or tunnel systems deep within the Earth. The North Germans and Scandinavians called this area the Land of the Nibelungen, or Niebelungen. In Wagner's opera by this name, we find the Dwarf Alberich, or Albrich, who was the guardian of the underwater treasure. These beings are wary of humans, but some of them will sometimes come into a human home during bad weather to hold their festivals in comfort. If the humans are polite, they may even be asked to join the Dwarfs. If the humans are rude or reject the invitation, the Dwarfs will see that misfortune comes to the household.

DWARF

Because the Dwarfs work so closely with the vibrations of the Earth itself, they have an immense amount of power over its rocks, including the mineral parts of animals and humans. They primarily work with stones, gems, and metals, and are considered to be the guardians of hidden treasures. They take great pride in the cutting of crystals and the development of veins of ore.

The most descriptive stories of the magickal abilities of the Dwarfs with metals is in the myths of the Norse. The beings can work metals into any kind of weapon or jewelry. On several occasions, the Dwarfs made valuable magickal objects for the gods, including Odhinn's spear and ring, Freyja's necklace and magickal sow, and Freyr's boat, which could be folded and put in a pocket.

The Abbe de Villars believed, and wrote, that the Earth is filled with more Dwarfs than we imagine, that they are ingenious creatures and ordinarily friendly toward humans. Other writers disagree about their amiability, calling them tricky, malicious, and treacherous. They all agree, though, that once you win the confidence and trust of a Dwarf, he is a faithful friend.

Folklore says that human miners sometimes accidentally broke into an underground workshop belonging to the Dwarfs or into one of the seams of ore they too were exploiting. If the miners greeted these beings politely, there was no problem; the Dwarfs might even point the way to another ore pocket.

Although some people believe the Dwarfs have no written language, this is not true. They use their written language only when engraving protective charms on objects they forge or in sending rare messages. However, their oral tradition is excellent; certain Dwarfs have the duty to remember and recall upon need the entire history of their specific colony and the major events of Dwarf culture in general.

In Gotho-Germanic mythology there are stories of the Duergar, a small people who lived in rocks and hills. They were said to have short legs and arms which nearly came to the ground when they stood upright. Experts in metallurgy, the Duergar worked in gold, silver, iron, and any other metal. They are particularly skilled in the making of arms and armor. Legend says that to get one of their creations through stealing, coercion, or violence brought bad luck. The people of Finland believed that Dwarfs were basically friendly to humans if treated with respect and kindness.

Icelandic Dwarfs wear red clothes, while those of Gudmandstrup, Zealand, dress in long black robes. The Dwarfs living around Ebeltoft are said to have humps on their backs and long crooked noses; they wear gray jackets and red pointed hats.

On the Baltic Sea island of Rugen, the people believed in three kinds of Dwarfs, whom they called Black, White, and Brown. The White were said to be beautiful and very gentle, spending the winter within their hill-homes forging fine objects of gold and silver. During the summer they often came out at night to dance around the hills and brooks.

The Brown Dwarfs were said to be only eighteen inches tall and could become any size they desired. These Dwarfs dressed all in brown with a little silver bell on their caps; they wore glass shoes. They also were very beautiful with light-colored eyes. They too danced in the moonlight and could become invisible whenever they wished. Good-natured beings, these Dwarfs loved children and often protected them.

The Black Dwarfs were said to be malicious and unfriendly toward humans. They were ugly and wore black jackets and caps. However, they were experts in the working of metals, particularly steel. These Dwarfs kept close to their hill-homes, coming out only to sit under elder trees; they did not sing or dance. No more than two or three of them gathered at one time.

The Hindu deity called Kubera fits the description of a Dwarf. An ugly but bejewelled being, he is the guardian of the northern direction. He lives in the Himalayas, where he is said to guard the treasures of the Earth. Kubera is portrayed as a small being with three legs and only eight teeth, who carries a sack over his shoulder and a casket in his right hand. When it is necessary for him to travel, he uses his aerial chariot named Pushpaka.

Psychological Attributes: A person who delights in being out in Nature, loves plants and animals; a lover of jewelry and personal adornment.

Magickal Attributes: Dwarfs—Working with crystals and gems; prosperity; working with metals; jewelry-making. Kubera—Fertility, treasure, mineral wealth, jewelry, gold, silver, gems and precious stones, and pearls. However, he is also considered to be the deity of thieves.

Elves

The word Elf comes from the Scandinavian and North Germanic words *aelf/ylf* (masculine) and *aelfen/elfen* (feminine).[1] Many Elves and Faeries are associated with the East and the Element of Air. Their leader is commonly known by the name Paralda. The species known as Elves is basically the caretakers of trees and forests. Although most Elves are helpful and benevolent toward friendly humans, their character depends upon the country in which they live. In Germany, for instance, Elves are treated with much caution because of their occasional malicious temperament.

Although Elves are grouped with Faeries in the Element of Air, they are different in temperament, looks, actions, and lifestyle. The most accurate description of Elves can be found in Tolkien's books, a far cry from the usual nonsensical way Elves are perceived to be.

Elves can come in many sizes, from much smaller than humans to human stature. Some of them are able to change size at will, even taking on a more human appearance for short periods. They look much like humans, except they are much more beautiful and have slightly pointed ears and tipped eyes. Their skin coloring ranges from pale to nut-brown; their hair is white-blonde, dark chestnut brown, or black. Their eyes are very striking shades of green and woodland brown.

Paracelsus wrote that many Elves build homes out of what looks like alabaster or marble, but which in reality have no physical counterpart on our plane of existence. Even Socrates, whose words were preserved by Plato in his *Phaedo,* said they had palaces and sacred places. Elfin society is based on ancient traditional lines, with a king and queen.

They can live up to a thousand years, with age only becoming apparent near the end of their life. Elves are usually capable of great humor, have vast stores of ancient knowledge, and make themselves known only to humans whom they consider worthy of their time and trust.

A long time ago people talked about Elf-books, which were books given to people the Elves loved for the purpose of helping them foretell the future.

Although Elves have great wisdom, can see into the future, and take their positions in life very seriously, they are not always solemn. They have festivals and cele-

ELVISH HARPER

brations where they dance, sing, and feast from dusk until dawn. When the first cock crows to announce the morning, the Elves instantly vanish, leaving only their footprints in the dew on the grass. Old traditions say that humans should not get close to Elves dancing in the moonlight, or they will vanish with these beings when the Sun rises. Elves can become invisible whenever they wish.

In Danish tales, the Elves were called the Elle-people. The men were always said to appear old and wore low-crowned hats, while the women were very beautiful and young, but were hollow behind. They raised large blue cattle.

However, there are a few Elves who prefer a more solitary life, living in or near the trees with which they work. One would assume that the solitary Elves take on some of the basic appearance of, or appearances which correspond to, their chosen tree. European tradition says, for example, that Elves who nurture and guard the poisonous hemlock resemble tiny human skeletons, thinly covered with semi-transparent flesh.

There is also a classification of Elves sometimes called dusky or dark Elves. This particular type of being is not friendly toward humans, but they seldom cause harm. However, the country people of Scandinavia believed that the dark Elves could cause sickness or injury; when this happened, the people called on a Kloka man (Wise man), who was especially trained to deal with such problems. The dark Elves prefer dark, gloomy places, sometimes setting up residence in basements and other such earth-linked structures. They will project negative energy toward humans, making them feel uncomfortable. Many people think they have ghosts in their home when the spooky feeling really comes from dark Elves.

In Germany the Wilde Frauen (Wild-Women) can be found, who seem to be related to the elves. They are very beautiful and have long flowing hair. Ordinarily they are seen alone or in the company of other Wild-Women. Tradition says that Wild-Women live within the hollow interior of the Wunderberg (or Underberg), a huge mountain on the moor near Salzburg. Deep inside the Wunderberg are palaces, gardens, sacred areas for worship, and springs.

In Japan live similar little Elfin-like beings called Chin-Chin Kobakama. These appear as small elderly, but spry, men and women who are active only during the day. They are benevolent toward humans, but can be a nuisance as they are extremely particular about the house being kept clean. As long as they are content, they will protect and bless the house and its occupants. If they feel the humans are not doing a good job, they will not hesitate to harass them and make life miserable in dozens of little ways.

Hindu mythology also mentions Elves; they call them the Ribhus. These creatures were the sons of Indra by Saranyu, the daughter of Tvashtri. They were artisans. The Ribhus are concerned with herbs, crops, streams, creativity, and blessings.

In the forests of northern Italy are solitary wood Elves known as Gianes [gee-ahwn-ayes]. They dress in old-fashioned clothing and wear pointed hats; in their back pockets they carry a small spinning wheel which they can use to see into the future. Although these beings are experts at weaving spells through the spinning of their wheels, they will not do spells for humans, but instruct them on how to do spells for themselves.

Psychological Attributes: A seeker of knowledge, especially the ancient kind. A person who seeks knowledge of the use of herbs and the Earth powers.

Magickal Attributes: Foretelling; the arts; creativity; herbs, crops, streams, woodlands. Seeking an astral lover; learning ancient secrets and knowledge.

Wise and tall Elven sage
Grant me in this common age
To teach me of the secrets old
and ancient knowledge left untold

Fox Spirits

The Japanese and Chinese have a number of stories about Fox Spirits, or Fox Faeries. Sometimes the spirit of a fox possesses a human; other times, after reaching a certain age, the fox itself is able to assume human form, usually as a beautiful woman. Fox Spirits are masters of illusion and love to trick humans. They have also been known to haunt places. Distance or security is no barrier if they want to steal something. They can live for centuries, even reincarnating if they are killed. It is believed that the Fox Spirits have a magick pearl, which they carry in their mouths or tucked under their tails.

There is one sign you can look for if you think you have met a Fox Spirit. A psychic person will be able to see a little point of flame over the being's head. To make the Fox Spirit resume its own shape and break its spell, one should attempt to get it to look into still water; water will reflect the fox image, breaking the illusion. Another method is for this mischievous spirit to hear a barking dog.

However, if the Fox Spirit is over 1,000 years old, a barking dog will have no effect. The only way to break the spell of a Fox Spirit this old is to entice it into the light of a fire made of wood as old as it is. An ancient spirit such as this will have white or golden fur, instead of the usual reddish color. It may even have nine tails. Although its magickal power is at its peak, a Fox Spirit of this great age seldom plays tricks on humans anymore.

In China these supernatural spirits are said to be able to cause continued accidents and misfortune in certain houses or villages. It is assumed that humans have annoyed or upset the spirits to such a degree that the foxes decided to retaliate. Steps are sometimes taken to exorcise the

FOX SPIRIT

Fox Spirit. Or, as not all Fox Spirits are bad or evil, a more common method is to make them comfortable by building them a little house of their own and stocking it with food and incense.

In Japan the Fox Spirit was considered a deity, in particular a rice spirit. Inari, the fox-goddess, is also called the "spirit of the rice." She has a main temple at Kyoto, but there are a great many smaller shrines in temples and private homes throughout the country.

In ancient Lydia, one form of Dionysus was that of a fox. When the Greek god assumed this aspect, he was called Bassareus. His fox-skin-wearing priestesses were known as Bassarids.

Psychological Attributes: One who rarely gets caught by the mind-games of others, but is adept at playing those games nonetheless.

Magickal Attributes: Tricky to work with; all rituals calling upon Fox Spirits must be done with great care. Crops, wild animals.

Gnomes

Gnomes are elemental beings who are closely tied to the Earth; the word Gnome may come from the Greek *genomus,* which means "earth dweller,"[2] or *gnoma,* which means "the knowing ones." The term Gnome has come to include many species of Earth elementals besides the creatures we know by this name.

The Germans call these little beings Erdmanleins, while in the German Alpine areas they are known as Heinzemannchens. The Swedes know them as the Nissen, a name similar to Nisse, which is used by the Danes and Norwegians. The Balkan countries have several names: Gnom, Djude, and Mano.

Gnomes themselves, as a species, are of a wide variety of types and forms. Most of them range from four to twelve inches in height. They take on the physical appearance of the people of the country and culture in which they live, and have been seen all around the world. The older males grow beards, while it is traditional for the married females to wear a scarf.

Most Gnomes weave cloth for clothing, sewing it into peasant costumes. Some of them wear clothing made from the plants near where they live, while others appear to "grow" their garments like the fur of animals. The males usually wear pointed red hats, multi-colored stockings or tight leg coverings, and a jerkin or tunic. The females wear head-scarves, blouses, long skirts, aprons, and multi-colored stockings.

Gnomes can live for several hundred years. They marry and have families. Small children of a quiet disposition often see and communicate with Gnomes, while this is more difficult for adults, who question everything.

Most Gnomes are prepared to earn their food by diligent work. Their usual foods are cereals and root vegetables, but for special festive occasions they do brew ale. Ordinarily, they are good-humored beings, helpful and benign to humans and all other creatures. However, if humans destroy their habitat with reckless regard, they have been known to sabotage projects and cause great damage. Gnomes prefer to build underground colonies in dim forests or the root systems of large trees. They are adaptable, though, and will build homes in rock gardens, empty bird houses, thick shrubbery, or other out-of-the-way places in civilization. They often have several secret hiding places where they can store things.

Gnomes are not fond of technology, preferring to work at their weaving and woodworking or helping the plants and animals that share their environment. Since they have great insight into actions of universal energy, they can influence animate and inanimate creatures and objects. To raise magickal energy, the Gnomes like to dance.

Gnomes have an innate ability to learn from the past and predict the future. They also have great understanding of the energy patterns around all things, making it possible for them to influence and heal. Seldom are Gnomes malicious or troublesome.

A very similar being in Denmark and Sweden is called the Nisse god-dreng (Nisse good lad), and in Sweden the Tomtgubbe (Old Man of the House). They say the Nisse is about the size of a year-old child, but looks like an old man dressed in gray with a pointed red cap. They say nothing goes well unless a Nisse lives in the house or on the farm. The Norwegian Nisse love the moonlight and, during the winter, often frolic in the snow at night; they are highly skilled in fiddling, music, and dance. Nisse who live in churches are called the Kirkegrim.

Psychological Attributes: A happy person who likes to aid animals. One close to the Earth and the Old Gods, especially the Goddess.

Magickal Attributes: Good luck, fiddle-playing, music, dance, divination, raising magickal energy, help for plants or animals.

Goblins

Tradition says that Goblins entered France through the Pyrenees mountains. They later spread throughout Europe. By stowing away on the Viking dragonships, they entered Britain, where they were given the name Robin Goblin, which was later shortened to Hobgoblin. The Germans call these troublesome beings Gobelins; to the Scots they are Brags.

Like many other Earth spirits, the Goblins have a human-like form, but there is only a slight family connection between them and Gnomes, Pixies, Gremlins, Elves, Leprechauns, and Faeries. The other Earth spirits will not allow them in their company because of the Goblin tendency for malicious mischief and evil cunning. Tradition says that originally Goblins were not the troublesome, hateful beings they are now, but were a more shaggy form of Brownie. Then the Goblins began to associate closely with some of the more undesirable humans and learned their devious ways.

Some of the Goblins can change their size, ranging from very small to almost human-sized. They can appear to humans as only a dark blob, or they can suddenly materialize with mean looks on their faces. Instead of the appealing smiles of Gnomes, Goblins have wide grins that can raise the hair on your neck. Their coloring is in all shades of browns, and some of them are quite hairy. They have stubby ears and eyes that glitter with malice. They are extremely strong and most active at night.

Their abilities in mischief-making are in the areas of luck-spoiling and weaving nightmares. That is not the extent of their mischief-making, though. They love to tip over pails, hide things, blow soot down the chimney or dirt in your face, alter sign posts, and blow out candles in scary-places. Fortunately, Goblins are not interested in tools and machinery.

GOBLIN

Folk tales say that the smile of a Goblin will curdle the blood, while his laugh will sour milk and make fruit fall from the trees. Even magicians will not allow a Goblin to stay around, because it is such a nuisance.

Goblins can easily communicate with such noxious creatures as flies, wasps, mosquitoes, and hornets. During the summer they like nothing better than to send these troublesome insects in hordes toward warm-blooded creatures, then laugh at the results.

Goblins have no homes as we think of homes, mainly because they do not tend to settle in one place for long. They will temporarily take shelter in mossy clefts in rocks and the twisting surface roots of old trees. The squeals and shrill tittering of a Goblin gang is a warning that they are in the neighborhood.

In Scotland, a malicious, ill-tempered close relative of the Goblin is known as a Boggart. In areas of northern England, this hateful creature is called a Padfoot or Hobgoblin. This solitary male being appears as short and ugly with distorted features. He only comes into a house to create trouble and destroy things. Most active at night, the Boggart enjoys tormenting and terrifying children, but will not hesitate to play his favorite trick of wrapping the blankets about the head of a sleeping adult and then laughing uproariously when the person awakens half-smothered. If they have been exorcised from a house, they will take up residence along a road and frighten passersby.

Psychological Attributes: A malicious type of person who enjoys frightening and/or terrorizing others.

Magickal Attributes: Not recommended. Once inside your home or ritual circle, Goblins (like Bogies) are difficult to get rid of.

Gremlins

Although distantly related to the craftsman Gnome and the mischievous Goblins, Gremlins are primarily Earth spirits who love to tinker with tools and machinery. At one time they were thought to be friendly with humans, showing them how to make better and more efficient tools, sharing new inventions, and inspiring better craftsmanship. The friendship soured when humans took credit for the Gremlins' work. Some people think that Gremlins only came to life during World War II when reports coupled them with airplane problems. However, these little beings have been around since humans first began to use any implement, other than a branch or rock, to help them with their work.

Now the Gremlins try to make life as miserable for humans as they can. They like nothing better than to make paint run down your arm, get you to saw through a knot in a plank, or hit your thumb with a hammer. Holding down the lever on the toaster so the toast burns sends them into howls of laughter. So does letting the air out of a tire when you are late for work. They are experts at choking the fuel line on the lawn mower or playing with the hot and cold water while you are taking a shower. Gremlins never run out of ideas to torment humans in little ways. Gremlins prefer to live in homes or buildings where there is lots of machinery in one form or another. Tradition says that there is at least one Gremlin in every household or business.

Psychological Attributes: One with an inventive mind or the ability to work with and repair machinery. Rather unsociable.

Magickal Attributes: Not recommended. Gremlins tend to cause enough trouble without deliberately inviting them into magickal workings.

Knockers

Knockers are underground beings who have made contact with miners since the Phoenicians first came to Cornwall to barter for tin, silver, copper, and lead. At one time they were found only in Cornwall, but have since traveled as far as Australia, where they are called Knackers.

Sightings of Knockers are rare, but it is said that they resemble Gnomes. Usually all a miner glimpses is a trickle of pebbles as the Knocker quickly passes by, or tiny footprints, which rapidly disappear, in damp earth at the bottom of a shaft.

These subterranean beings are helpful to miners, warning them of danger or directing them to a vein of ore. These warnings or directions always come in the form of mysterious knocking sounds, hence their name. Some miners are better than others at deciphering these knocks. When Cornish miners have been warned by wild knocking of a coming disaster, such as a mine collapse, explosion, or flooding, they will refuse to return to the pits. These miners will not whistle, swear, or make the sign of the cross while down in the mines, as the Knockers do not like this kind of behavior. The Knockers have led searchers to trapped miners on many occasions by continually knocking just ahead of the search party until the correct place is reached.

In Wales these subterranean beings are called Coblynaus. They are about a foot and a half tall and dress like the miners. It is considered very lucky to hear them, although they will throw stones if ignored or mocked. In Germany these beings are known as Wichlein; in southern France as Gommes.

Psychological Attributes: A person who has learned to dig into the subconscious and superconscious minds for spiritual treasure.

Magickal Attributes: Help in mining and prospecting.

Kobolds

Every household should have a Kobold in residence. Kobolds are useful and can be very helpful in exchange for a little regular offering. However, one should make certain that they are the friendly type, not the troublesome ones who act like poltergeists.

In Finland the Kobold was called the Para. Although the Finlanders made pacts with them, offering food and shelter in return for prosperity, they said the Kobolds were known for creating mischief. Once in

KOBOLD

a house, this type of Kobold was said to be notoriously difficult to remove. Some churches in Finland kept exorcists whose primary job was to expel unwanted Kobolds.

Kobold is a German word meaning Goblin. The German silver miners believed that Kobolds liked to live in the mines, and oftentimes, especially if offended, would poison the ore to make the miners sick.

Kobolds are rarely seen by humans. Those who have been fortunate enough to see these creatures describe them as little old men with wrinkled faces, wearing brown knee pants and red felt hats and smoking pipes. They will work tirelessly for a household which shows its appreciation. They enjoy creating a pleasant atmosphere of luck and ease, making the chores go smoothly and the garden grow better. If not shown appreciation for their efforts, Kobolds can make you drop dishes, trip, or burn your fingers.

The Kobolds who are not so friendly toward humans can be very troublesome. If they feel they have been ignored or insulted, and sometimes just because they feel like it, they will make all kinds of noise and throw things around the room.

Psychological Attributes: A person who tends to be very troublesome and vocal at imagined slights.

Magickal Attributes: Good luck; help in making things run smoothly. Be certain you specify only the helpful Kobolds, not the poltergeist ones.

Ohdows

These mysterious little beings are part of the Native American culture. The Ohdows are a tribal species that lives underground and has never been seen. The Native Americans say they are very small but not deformed in any way, looking much like the Indian tribes.

The Ohdows have strong magickal powers which they use to benefit animals, humans, and the Earth itself. Their primary task is to control gigantic evil spirits who live deep within the planet and who would devastate the Earth and destroy everything on it. These evil spirits have but one goal: to get to the surface and wreak havoc. The Ohdows use their magick powers to keep these spirits locked within their subterranean caverns. From time to time the evil spirits beat against the cavern walls, creating angry rumblings and deep terrifying noises. This lasts until the Ohdows can overcome them and cause them to sleep once more.

Psychological Attributes: One close to Earth energies; a person who can predict natural disasters.

Magickal Attributes: Protection from earthquakes and other earthly disasters.

Old Lady of the Elder

Many cultures believe that elder trees have certain magickal powers and that they are strengthened and protected by a strange species of Earth being called the Old Lady of the Elder. In Scandinavian countries this being is called the Hyldermoder (Elder Mother). In Germany and parts of Denmark it is still a common custom among the country folk to tip one's hat when passing an elder tree.

The Old Lady is rarely seen by humans. However, the best times for a glimpse of her are in the spring when the elder trees are covered with white flowers and again in the autumn when the blackberries ripen. She likes to be out and about, especially when the Moon is full. The Old Lady of the Elder appears as an elderly lady dressed in a black apron with a white cap and shawl. With her gown the color of elder tree bark, she can move almost invisibly through the shadows under the trees. She hobbles along using a gnarled staff cut from an elder branch.

Tradition says that the Old Lady imparts magickal power to the elder, some of which can be tapped by humans for white magick, some for black magick. A number of salves and potions can be made from the flowers, berries, or bark. Wands, rune sticks, and other ritual items can be fashioned from the wood itself, but the tree must always be asked before cutting and a gift of milk and honey left in thanks.

Using elder wood for mundane purposes, though, is not considered to be a wise act. If the wood is used for a cradle, for example, traditions says the child will be sickly; if used for furniture, it will quickly split and collapse; if used for roof beams, the house will never know good luck.

Psychological Attributes: Encouraging Moon magick to grow within yourself; one who seeks to understand and use magick of both the Full and Dark Moons.

Magickal Attributes: Gaining wisdom about herbs; creating wands and ritual items.

Pixies

These small creatures at one time inhabited the far western sections of England, especially Cornwall. Where they originated, no one knows. Tradition says there has always been enmity between Pixies and Faeries, which sometimes erupts into battles. Another name for Pixies is Piskies. Their mischievous behavior has given us the word *pesky.*

Pixies are about the size of a human hand, but have the ability to increase or decrease their size whenever they wish. Their most noticeable characteristics are their bright red hair, green eyes, pointed ears, and turned-up noses. Both males and females wear close-fitting outfits of bright green, which act as a camouflage when they are out in the fields and forests. Often they are seen wearing a hat made of a foxglove blossom or a toadstool, two plants they dearly love. They love flowering gardens and herb beds. They, like many similar beings, are active at Beltane when they gather at Pixie Fairs to sing, dance, play, and make music.

Although these beings do not directly harm humans, they are

PIXIES

malicious tricksters who like nothing better than to lead humans astray when out hiking or traveling. They can confuse some humans so much that they never recover, but take to wandering aimlessly, singing and talking in unknown languages. In sections of English Pixie-country, this is known as "pixie led." Tradition says the only method known to work against the glamour of Pixies is to wear your coat inside-out.

It is not unknown for a Pixie, especially the males, to take on a full-grown human appearance in an attempt to cause trouble. If you see a man with squinting green eyes, bright red hair, and a mischievous smile, you should take care not to get involved in any of his schemes.

English farmers in Pixie-country try to avoid getting on the wrong side of Pixies. They do this by leaving out water for the Pixie mothers to wash their babies and keeping the hearth swept for Pixie dancing.

Psychological Attributes: One with a sense of humor that sometimes borders on the kind of humor that isn't funny.

Magickal Attributes: Very tricky to work with. Singing, dance, music.

Red Cap

The Red Cap is an evil goblin-like creature who lives along the border between England and Scotland. There, he takes up residence in ruined castles and ancient watchtowers. Sometimes he even lives in old piles of stones along the lonely border tracks. Because the Red Cap can be bound and exorcised, he frequently changes his place of residence to avoid people who are powerful enough to do this.

One should avoid looking for, or meeting, one of these dangerous creatures. He seeks human prey to renew the color of his bright cap in their blood. The Red Cap looks like a short, stocky old man with long gray hair and eagle's claws instead of hands. Although he wears iron boots, he can move very swiftly. Even from a distance, a Red Cap can be identified by his fiery red eyes and red hat.

There is only one method given in folk tales to defeat a Red Cap: the use of holy words. However, considering how the Christians rewrote everything, including folk tales, the "holy" words very likely were originally magick words. The proper words will make him unable to harm you, and he will disappear.

Psychological Attributes: The type of personality that seeks out "victims," whether of the emotions or the body.

Magickal Attributes: Extremely dangerous. Not recommended.

The Salamander

Salamanders are connected with the Element of Fire and the South; their leader is called Djinn. *Salambe* in Greek described a fireplace. These creatures are the most difficult for humans to contact. In fact, ancient magicians considered them extremely dangerous and issued strong warnings to their students to keep away from Fire Salamanders. There are no common grounds of thinking or working between these creatures and humans. However, one may see a Salamander by chance when gazing into a fire.

The Fire Salamander is described as similar to the black and yellow lizards which live in damp, mossy places in Britain and Europe. The Salamander, however, lives in the center of fires, especially the hottest fires like volcanoes and lava. However, when incense is burned, one can find tiny Salamanders curling with the rising smoke. Some Salamanders can grow to a foot long.

Paracelsus, the Swiss philosopher, wrote that these Elementals could also be seen in small balls of light which danced over fields

SALAMANDER

and houses during storms. These creatures can also be found in St. Elmo's fire, the forks of strange flame seen on masts and rigging of ships at sea.

Although the Salamander is known to those in magick as a creature of the Element of Fire, it was also known to medieval peoples as the alchemist's lizard.

Psychological Attributes: A knowledgeable magician who has learned to work with magick of the Elements.

Magickal Attributes: Very dangerous. Not recommended unless you are an experienced, accomplished magician. Seeking out the most difficult and sometimes dangerous spiritual knowledge.

Trolls

These beings originally came from the Nordic and North Germanic countries, but now can be found in many places around the world. In Sweden they are called Trolds, while in Denmark they are known as Hill Men or Berg People.

Descriptions vary from gnome-size to giants; these are all correct as Trolls come in all sizes and shapes. Usually they are strange-looking beings, often indistinct in form, with barely any neck. Some of them are very tall and thin, while others are stockier. Their voices are deep and rumbling, similar to the sounds of rock slides. They are extremely strong, and most of them not too intelligent. However, a few are quite good at mechanics and working at the forge.

They prefer the mountains, deep forests, and moorlands and live underground or in dark enclosed places which are built into the Earth. Even the smallest hill can contain the home of a Troll, and often does. With human cities spreading as they are, it is now possible to see Trolls under highway overpasses, in abandoned brick or concrete buildings, or even peering up through storm drains.

Trolls are out more frequently at night and during the twilight hours of dusk. Tradition says they cannot tolerate the Sun and will turn to stone if it shines upon them. This may be because sunlight is incompatible with their cellular structure and/or internal make-up. Although they regularly wander the countryside at night, it can be quite difficult to find and see a Troll, as they can become invisible at will.

TROLL

The Scandinavians believe Trolls are antagonistic toward humans, stealing children and attacking any people they meet on their nightly strolls. For this reason, they will avoid going out at night or leaving the windows open. Their tales say that any human who sees a Troll will become addled in the mind. If a Troll gets too close to a farmstead, they say cats and dogs will hide, the hens will not lay, and the cows will not give milk.

Trolls often run in gangs and act like bullies, throwing rocks at humans (their favorite sport). They think humans smell bad and are very ugly.

The Illes [eels], a branch of the Troll family, live in Iceland. They also live underground, coming out only at night when they dance, sing, and play music for hours under a Full Moon. Although they are hairy and dark-colored, the Illes can shape-shift into attractive human-shapes with the intent of luring humans into their subterranean realm.

The people who live on the Feroes Islands call Trolls the Foddenskkmaend, Underground-People, or Hollow Men. They fear the Trolls, for tradition says they carry humans into their hill-homes and keep them there.

Psychological Attributes: Positive—One who uses physical strength and/or abilities in martial arts to defend the helpless. Negative—One who doesn't hesitate to use physical strength to bully others.

Magickal Attributes: Take care in working with Trolls; they can be dangerous and troublesome. They will appear without being called if they feel you are ready to work with them. If you meet and work with Trolls in an amiable fashion, not trying to command them, they can provide protection and let you into the secrets concerning the magick of mountains (even small ones). Music, song, dance, mechanics, working with metals, protection.

Uldra or Huldra-Folk

Although many writers claim that the Scandinavian Uldra and the Huldra-Folk are the same beings, there appear to be differences. Perhaps this is because certain branches of the species have developed different traits.

According to Simak, by the late Middle Ages the idea of Elves and Dwarfs had merged into the Huldra-Folk. I believe that Simak is mistaken in this, however, as there is little resemblance between Elves, Dwarfs, and the Huldra-Folk.

In some ways the Huldra-Folk superficially resemble Elves, Dwarfs, and Trolls. Some people even call them dark Elves and say they have nasty personalities. The Huldra-Folk do seem to have a blend of Elf and Dwarf traits, sometimes helping humans, sometimes playing tricks on them. However, the Laplanders, to whom it is said they still appear, separate them clearly from other Earth beings.

The Laplanders, a very ancient migratory culture whose lives revolve around their reindeer, live in the far north of Sweden. The Uldra (as the Lapps call them) are gentle Nature spirits, the Little People of this northern area. Their homes are said to be underground. They often come to the surface to work with the animals, particularly in winter when one of their tasks is to feed hibernating bears and other sleeping creatures.

The Uldra adults are rarely seen, but the little babies, who are curious about humans, sometimes wander close to Lapland camps. The children have long sharp teeth and their faces are covered with black hair.

The Norwegians refer to the Huldra-Folk as a kind of Elf that lives in caves and small hills. They sometimes call them the Hogfolk (Hill-People).

ULDRA CHILD

These beings are said to be very beautiful and sing and play music on warm summer nights. One of their tunes, called the Elf-king's tune, although known to a few old fiddlers, is never played, for once begun the fiddler cannot stop unless someone cuts the strings on his instrument. This tune also is said to compel all animate and inanimate objects to dance as long as the fiddler plays.

The Bjergfolk, or Hill-People, of Scandinavia are often called Trolls, but they do not fit the usual description. Instead they resemble the Huldra-Folk, also called the Hill-People. They live in family or clan homes inside hills and mounds. These beings have magnificent homes decorated with gold and crystal, and sometimes are considered to be very rich. Usually the Hill-People are quite friendly toward humans, but on occasion they have been known to steal women and children. They particularly dislike the sound of bells. They have the ability to become invisible, shape-shift, tell the future, or cast spells of prosperity or bad luck.

Psychological Attributes: One who prefers solitude and Nature to the busy pace of social activities.

Magickal Attributes: Music, singing, dance, divination; casting prosperity spells; learning to become invisible or appearing to take the shape of someone or something else.

Winged Panthers

Leopards in the Middle and Far East were known as panthers. In Greece, the panther was an animal of Dionysus. Its name in Greek means "All-beast," possibly a reference to Dionysus as "God of the All." However, this same title was also applied to the god Pan.

Winged Panthers appear in ancient artwork, statues, and bas-reliefs mainly in the Near and Far East. One Nepalese stone statue of a Winged Panther portrays the creature with feathers or fur on the front and back legs and a feathery crest on top of its head. A piece of embroidery from Java shows the Winged Panther with wings, feathers, or flames coming from the back of all four legs; it has a feathery or flaming tail and a similar crest on its head; its body is covered with rosettes. However, on a ceramic jug from the Islam era, 1215–1216, of Kashan, a Winged Panther is shown with a human head and a panther body covered with rosettes.

The Underwater Panthers of the Native Americans might be considered a type of Winged Panther, although they were never described as having wings. These Panthers lived deep under water and, although said to be evil and devious, were also acknowledged as having powerful healing knowledge.

Psychological Attributes: One who lives with confidence, but is quite able to protect him or herself and family with whatever type of magick or personal defense is necessary.

Magickal Attributes: Very dangerous; not recommended unless you are an experienced, accomplished magician. A source of great wisdom and healing power, particularly with herbs. A guide and teacher of great ancient wisdom.

ENDNOTES

1. Rudolf Simak. *Dictionary of Northern Mythology.*
2. Manly P. Hall. *The Secret Teachings of All Ages.*

20

Summary

Not everyone who reads this book, or hears about it, will understand or relate to Otherworld beings in the same way I do. I have never insisted that another person must believe as I do. Everyone must discover the path of understanding that is right for him or her and best fits his or her present stage of development.

I have seen and talked with beings from the Otherworld for as long as I can remember. Usually these times of seeing or communication were intermittent, probably because of the unpleasant, condemning conditions under which I lived for years. However, as I began to form boundaries beyond which I allowed no family or friends to criticize, these beings became more common in my life.

At first these Otherworld beings just dropped in for visits, then left. However, after several years of this, a few started to become semi-permanent residents.

About 1985 a leprechaun began to visit us. He has lived with us for several years now, moving with us from one place to another. He comes and goes as he pleases, making his presence known by the smell of tobacco smoke from his pipe and the faint humming of Irish tunes.

Dragons, Faeries, Elves, and other beings often showed up during magickal workings and especially at the Solstices and Equinoxes. They became such common visitors that we ceased to be surprised at their appearances. But after I began researching for this book, a number of unexpected things happened.

First came the baby Troll. We had to replace the shelf under the sink as the previous house owners had allowed a leak which ruined it. It was a problem keeping two curious cats out of the space while we worked. They rumbled in and out under the sink most of the day without hesitation. As night came, however, the larger cat (who fears no one and nothing except the vacuum) started to go under the sink again, shot backward about two feet, and his hair went up. The little cat took one look under the sink from a distance and with an air of great dignity left the kitchen.

Curious, I peeked under the sink. In a shadowy back corner was a little Troll. It sat with its knees drawn up, one finger in its mouth, and its eyes wide. Since we live on a hillside, I shouldn't have been surprised that Trolls were in the neighborhood. Curiosity must have gotten the best of the baby Troll, who innocently wandered inside to see what we humans were doing. We carefully avoided the kitchen until the baby crept back out the cat-door to its mother.

Brown Knobbie is a Gnome who appeared one night in a particular corner of my office. He is so quiet and unobtrusive that often I am not aware he is there until I see one of the cats staring into that corner and holding a telepathic conversation with him. He never lets me see him straight on, but will come up beside me when I am working at the computer. His presence is always one of love, happiness, and willingness to help.

At Winter Solstice in 1994 a close friend sent a gift of a Gargoyle. This creature felt very much "alive" as I unwrapped him. We were delighted and set him on the dining table until we could decide where to place him. Our cat Callie has a habit of sitting on the table in the evening to watch my husband work. Since she had inspected the Gargoyle's box and wrappings, we were not prepared for what happened. That night Callie hopped onto the table and found herself face to face with the Gargoyle. Instantly her hair went up and she dropped into a crouch. She slowly crept up, nose to nose, with the statue. After a few moments of extremely careful inspection, she jumped off the table and has carefully ignored this particular Gargoyle ever since. She likes the other Gargoyle so much I have to keep her from licking him.

This Gargoyle has the amazing ability to make his "statue" invisible if he wishes. I'm amazed at how few people ever see the statue, even though it sits in plain sight facing the front door.

One day as I sat at my desk, a flash of green light crossed my peripheral vision, a strange occurrence as my office is painted white. Then in my right ear came the voice of Green Leaf, an Elf I've seen many times in ritual and meditation: "Why don't you tell how we really are instead of that sappy image?" As I was recovering from this sudden communication, close by my left ear a deep gravelly voice said, "And we're a lot more than bloody rain spouts, you know."

The second voice was unknown to me, but the Gargoyle to whom it belonged introduced himself as Ridkin. When I repeated the name, the Gargoyle laughed (it sounded like a voice at the bottom of a very deep well) and informed me the name was a play on words: Rid Kin. His presence is appreciated since I have several relatives who are always trying to nose into my personal affairs and are unsupportive of my religious practices.

The only reason I can find for being blessed with the presence of these Otherworld creatures is that my mind was open to all possibilities through my research, studies, and thoughts. Like most humans, helpful Otherworld beings will not go where they are not wanted, acknowledged, or appreciated.

If one wishes to make contact, however slight, with any of the magickal, mythical, mystical beings, one must have an open mind, be curious and aware, and be willing to learn new ways of communication and doing things, especially magick.

Humans need to recognize that there are other Worlds besides this physical one in which we exist. Just as if we were visiting a strange country on Earth, we must accept the ways of Otherworld beings as natural and right for them. We need to travel within these Otherworlds and meet Otherworld beings without giving offense or judging them. Politeness goes a lot further and gets a lot more help than orders and commands would.

May you learn to open your mind to all the wonderful possibilities of communication and cooperation with Otherworld magickal, mythical, mystical beings.

PART III

WORKING WITH MAGICK

21

Candle Burning

The burning of candles for a specific purpose is the easiest of all magickal practices. It is excellent for beginners and even advanced practitioners of magick who need to get things moving in a hurry and don't have the time or opportunity to do a complete ritual at that particular moment.

The most commonly used candles are unscented, about six inches long, and of the taper or square-end variety. Since you will usually be allowing them to burn completely out, you should also have metal or non-flammable holders with flared bases wide enough to catch dripping wax.

There is one basic rule in candle burning: for reversing or removing, burn during the waning Moon (after Full Moon until New Moon); for increasing or obtaining, burn during the waxing Moon (after New Moon until Full Moon). The

New Moon has the strongest power of the waning cycle, and the Full Moon has the strongest power during the waxing cycle.

To do a candle burning spell, select a color which represents the goal you have in mind and the mythical creature that you want to aid you. Carve or scratch your desire, using a few words, into the candle. Then hold it in both hands and mentally pour thoughts of your desired goal into the candle. When ready, set it into the holder and light it. Put it in a safe place to burn out completely.

Candles are often used in conjunction with chants, oils, herbs, and stones,[1] all geared toward one particular purpose. These add to the power of the candle. Candles can be rubbed with oil, then rolled in crushed herbs. Stones can be set in a circle around the burning candle. Chants can be said over the candles. Candle burning can also be part of a larger, more formal, and more involved ritual.

If rubbing the candle with oil, rub the oil onto the candle from the end to the wick to remove something from your life, or from the wick down to the end to draw something into your life.

Once you have lighted the candle, you can chant a little verse or piece of your own creation to help attract the particular magickal creature you have in mind.

The following list of candle colors will help you decide what colors to use.

Black: Binding; defense by repelling dark magick; transforming spells and thoughtforms into positive power; general defense; getting rid of pessimism and feeling bound.

Blue, Dark: Removing depression; changing impulsiveness; deep and strong changes in spiritual life.

Blue, Light: Harmony; understanding; journeys or moves; healing. Water Elementals.

Brown: Success with jobs, projects, or creative endeavors; gaining common sense; amplifying all Earth magick and psychic abilities. The color brown is used for down-to-earth projects, not inventions, projects of a mental nature, or anything to do with the emotional nature. Earth Elementals.

Gold: Money; prosperity; total success. Any creature connected with the Sun.

Gray or Silver: Deep spiritual seeking; standing in a neutral position in order to see behind illusion; seeking a high spiritual initiation. Any creature connected with the Moon.

Green: Marriage; relationships; balance; practical creativity, particularly with the hands; fertility; growth; attracting good luck; improving finances. Beings such as Elves, Gnomes, Brownies, and Faeries.

Indigo: Discovering past lives; searching out causes of karmic problems; balancing karma; stopping undesirable habits or experiences.

Lavender: Preparing for spiritual initiation; letting go of tension; learning to balance ambition; seeking out ancient knowledge.

Magenta: A color burned with other candles to speed up results. Very fast-acting.

Orange: Changing your luck; developing power; getting control of a situation; gaining confidence.

Pink: Healing emotional problems; true love; friendship; healing mental and emotional troubles.

Purple: Breaking bad luck; protection; psychic and spiritual growth; success in long-range plans; progress in business. Whenever using a purple candle, be sure your desires are of the highest spiritual intent, or you may suffer a backlash.

Red: Courage to face a conflict or test; energy; taking action; sexual love; learning to stand up for yourself. Fire Elementals.

White: Spiritual guidance; being directed into the right paths; calmness; becoming centered; seeing past all illusions.

Yellow: Developing power of the mind; creativity of a mental nature; sudden changes; being persuasive; gaining confidence. Air Elementals.

ENDNOTES

1. Any of Scott Cunningham's books (see Bibliography) are excellent references for the uses of oils, herbs, and stones in magick.

22

Amulets and Talismans

Amulets and talismans are still used throughout the world, even by so-called "sophisticated" society. The "lucky" bowling shirt, a four-leaf clover, the Pagan five-point star, and the Christian cross all fall into this category. Anything you use consistently to ward off misfortune or bring luck can be an amulet or a talisman.

Some people are confused as to what the difference is between the two, and will use the words interchangeably. An amulet is something which gives you occult protection. A talisman is an item which attracts prosperity, love, a job, good luck, or something similar.[1] Lippman and Colin say that an amulet can do no harm, while a talisman can be constructed for evil. While it is true that an amulet is more a shield and a talisman an actively working charm, either could be constructed for evil if the magician making them is on a negative path and of low spiritual morals.

Making either an amulet or talisman is neither difficult nor expensive. The power of these "charms" does not come from precious metals, impossible ingredients, or weeks of work. Rather it comes from the intense desire and/or need of the individual creating them.

The popular charm bracelet, still worn today, originally came from the ancient wearing of charmed objects on the body. At first these were worn about the neck on thongs or chains. Later, when the practice was frowned upon by Christians who wanted everyone to wear their cross instead, these charms were inconspicuously added to bracelets and brooches. The charms were usually a depiction of a mythical creature, some emblem symbolizing them, or a powerful Pagan symbol.

The Christian church leaders did with the mythical creatures as they did with so much else of the old Pagan beliefs: they tried to change the original meanings and force them into the Christian mold. Some creatures, such as the Unicorn and the Griffin, they rewrote as symbols of their Christ. Others, such as the Gargoyles and Fauns, they changed to creatures helping their devil.

During the Middle Ages, books about these mythical creatures began to appear. These bestiaries, as they were called (some of them are still available today in reprints), were full of this misinformation and all written by church-sanctioned scholars.

The only way to call upon the true powers of these mythical creatures is to go beyond the Christian influence and discover what they originally represented. Then the magician can use their symbols or pictures as an aid in manifesting a desired result.

It is possible to buy charms or small pieces of jewelry made in the images of many of the fabulous mythical beasts. These can be "programmed" through magick for a specific purpose and worn as an amulet or talisman or used in magickal procedures.

However, one does not have to purchase such charms to have them be effective. They can be made by the person using them, whatever his or her level or lack of skill. The amulet or talisman can be drawn on paper and carried in one's pocket or purse, even pinned inside clothing. If you have absolutely no drawing skills, don't despair. Simply write out the name of the creature which you are asking for help.

If you want to go beyond the paper charm, you can use squares or rounds of thin wood or even the flat, smooth end of a metal can. Then, using paints, inks, or an engraving tool, put the name of the mythical creature and/or its image on your chosen material. The image might go on one side, with the name on the other. This type of charm is best used in candle burning or ritual, not worn or carried.

Sometimes symbols are easier to draw than the images. For example, a four-leaf clover could be used to represent the Brownies, wings and a horseshoe for Pegasus, a stylized bull's head with wings for the Shedu, or a fish for one of the Water-Folk. Whatever you use to identify the fabulous mythical creature you are asking to work with you, be sure the image or symbol has meaning for you.

To empower the "charm," take it to your altar and pass it through incense smoke, sprinkle it very lightly with consecrated water, and wave it through the heat above a candle's flame. Then, holding it in both your hands, chant a verse or piece which you have written, petitioning the particular magickal creature you have in mind. Ask for them to put some of their energy into the "charm" and thank them for helping you.

ENDNOTES

1. Doreen Valiente, in her book *Natural Magic,* has a whole chapter on this subject.

23

Rituals

Whenever I speak or write about rituals, I mean specific magickal workings done within a cast and protected circle. When working with many of the magickal, mythical beings listed in this book, it is safest to call upon them or their powers only when within such a circle.

When such a circle is cast around an altar (a table holding your magickal equipment), this invisible working area is consecrated and sealed by the clockwise sprinkling of blessed water and salt around the edges. Then trace (in the air) the edge of the circle with your forefinger, athame, or sword. Finish by carrying smoking incense about it. Finally, beginning in the East and moving clockwise, the four cardinal directions are called upon for protection.

These directional calls may be directed to the four Archangels (of Ceremonial magick), the Lords and Ladies (of Paganism), or the Four

Rulers of the Elements. Your choice of directional protectors should be based on your personal preferences.

This ritual activity seals out negative influences and enables you to contain raised magickal energy until you are ready to release it to go about its work.

When you have finished your spellworking, dismiss the four directional protectors and ritually open or disperse the circle. Never leave the cast circle without dismissing the four directions as this will leave the elemental energies and the powers of the magickal being upon which you called to bounce around your living space uncontrolled.

The ritual work you do after casting the circle and calling the protectors can be in any form or wording you wish. It is quite proper and even desirable that you write your own rituals. The following examples of casting and closing a circle and calling upon the four directions are given only as guidelines for those people who are new to magickal workings.

Casting the Circle

Take up your athame or sword. (Use your forefinger if you don't have these.) Beginning in the East, visualize blue flames coming from the ritual tool and drawing the circle around you. End in the East, overlapping the invisible line.

Have a small goblet or glass of water and a small amount of salt on a plate on your altar. Hold your power hand (the one you use most) over the water and say:

> *I bless you in the name of positive power.*

Hold your hand over the salt; say:

> *I bless you in the name of positive power.*

Add a pinch of salt to the water and swirl the glass gently three times clockwise. Lightly sprinkle the water mixture around the circle edges, beginning and ending in the East.

Carry burning incense around the circle in the same manner, beginning and ending in the East. Say:

> *This circle is sealed against all negative influence and power.*

Now is the time to call upon the four directional protectors. Examples follow.

Calling the Four Directions

ARCHANGELS

Go to the East; hold up your hand or athame in salute. Say:

I call upon You, Raphael, to protect and guide me.

Move to the South; hold up your athame. Say:

I call upon You, Michael, to protect and guide me.

In the West, hold up your athame and say:

I call upon You, Gabriel, to protect and guide me.

Go to the North, hold up your athame, and say:

I call upon You, Auriel, to protect and guide me.

LORDS AND LADIES

Go to the East; hold up your hand or athame in salute. Say:

Come, you Lords and Ladies of the East. I call upon you to help and protect me in this time of magick.

Move to the South; hold up your athame. Say:

Come, you Lords and Ladies of the South. I call upon you to help and protect me in this time of magick.

In the West, hold up your athame and say:

Come, you Lords and Ladies of the West. I call upon you to help and protect me in this time of magick.

Go to the North, hold up your athame, and say:

Come, you Lords and Ladies of the North. I call upon you to help and protect me in this time of magick.

ELEMENTAL KINGS

Go to the East; hold up your hand or athame in salute. Say:

> *Behold, Paralda, you elementals of Air. I do summon, stir, and call you up to witness this rite and to guard this circle.*

Move to the South; hold up your athame. Say:

> *Behold, Djinn, you elementals of Fire. I do summon, stir, and call you up to witness this rite and to guard this circle.*

In the West, hold up your athame and say:

> *Behold, Niksa, you elementals of Water. I do summon, stir, and call you up to witness this rite and to guard this circle.*

Go to the North, hold up your athame, and say:

> *Behold, Ghom, you elementals of Earth. I do summon, stir, and call you up to witness this rite and to guard this circle.*

Dismissing the Four Directions

ARCHANGELS

Go to the East; hold up your hand or athame in salute. Say:

> *Farewell, Raphael. My thanks and blessings.*

Move to the South; hold up your athame. Say:

> *Farewell, Michael. My thanks and blessings.*

In the West, hold up your athame and say:

> *Farewell, Gabriel. My thanks and blessings.*

Go to the North, hold up your athame, and say:

> *Farewell, Auriel. My thanks and blessings.*

LORDS AND LADIES

Go to the East; hold up your hand or athame in salute. Say:

> *Go in peace, Lords and Ladies of the East.*
> *My thanks and blessings.*

Move to the South; hold up your athame. Say:

> *Go in peace, Lords and Ladies of the South.*
> *My thanks and blessings.*

In the West, hold up your athame and say:

> *Go in peace, Lords and Ladies of the West.*
> *My thanks and blessings.*

Go to the North, hold up your athame, and say:

> *Go in peace, Lords and Ladies of the North.*
> *My thanks and blessings.*

ELEMENTAL KINGS

Go to the East; hold up your hand or athame in salute. Say:

> *Depart in peace, you elementals of Air. I give my thanks and say*
> *fare you well.*

Move to the South; hold up your athame. Say:

> *Depart in peace, you elementals of Fire. I give my thanks and say*
> *fare you well.*

In the West, hold up your athame, and say:

> *Depart in peace, you elementals of Water. I give my thanks and*
> *say fare you well.*

Go to the North, hold up your athame, and say:

> *Depart in peace, you elementals of Earth. I give my thanks and*
> *say fare you well.*

Closing the Circle

Using your forefinger, athame, or sword, go to the East and "cut" through the air counterclockwise on the edge of the circle. Say:

> *This circle is now open. The powers raised here go forth to create*
> *my desire. I give my thanks and blessings to all who have helped*
> *me here this night. May there be peace and love between us when-*
> *ever we meet again.*

Bibliography

Andrews, Ted. *Enchantment of the Faerie Realm*. St. Paul, MN: Llewellyn, 1993.

Ayto, John. *Arcade Dictionary of Word Origins*. NY: Arcade Publishing, 1990.

Baring-Gould, Sabine. *Curious Myths of the Middle Ages*. NY: University Books, 1967.

Barrett, W. H. *Tales from the Fens*. UK: Routledge & Kegan Paul, 1963.

Baumgartner, Anne S. *A Comprehensive Dictionary of the Gods*. NY: University Books, 1984.

Beagle, Peter S. *The Last Unicorn*. NY: Viking, 1968.

Beer, Robert Rudiger. Trans. by Charles M. Stern. *Unicorn: Myth & Reality*. UK: Van Nostrand Reinhold Co., 1977.

Beltz, Walter. *God & The Gods: Myths of the Bible*. UK: Penguin, 1983.

Bett, Henry. *English Myths & Traditions*. UK: Batsford, 1952.

Black, Jeremy and Green, Anthony. *Gods, Demons & Symbols of Ancient Mesopotamia.* Austin, TX: University of Texas Press, 1992.

Blanchard, Robert. *The Stone Missal: A Grimoire on the Magick of the Gargoyles.* Palm Springs, CA: International Guild of Occult Sciences, 1993.

Bowker, James. *Goblin Tales of Lancashire.* UK: Swan Sonnenschein, 1883.

Branston, Brian. *Gods of the North.* UK: Thames & Hudson, 1955.

Briggs, Katharine, ed. *British Folktales.* NY: Dorset Press, 1977.

Briggs, Katharine. *An Encyclopedia of Fairies, Hobgoblins, Brownies, Bogies, & Other Supernatural Creatures.* NY: Pantheon Books, 1976.

Briggs, Katharine. *The Fairies in Tradition & Literature.* UK: Routledge & Kegan Paul, 1967.

Briggs, Katharine. *The Vanishing People: Fairy Lore & Legends.* NY: Pantheon Books, 1978.

Brown, Robert. *Semitic Influence in Hellenic Mythology.* NY: Arno, 1977.

Budge, E. A. Wallis. *Amulets & Superstitions.* NY: Dover, 1978.

Budge, E. A. Wallis. *Dwellers on the Nile.* NY: Dover, 1977.

Budge, E. A. Wallis. *Gods of the Egyptians.* 2 vols. NY: Dover, 1969.

Bunting, Eve. *Night of the Gargoyles.*

Cavendish, Richard, ed. *Mythology: An Illustrated Encyclopedia.* NY: Rizzoli, 1980.

Christie, Anthony. *Chinese Mythology.* UK: Paul Hamlyn, 1973.

Cirlot, J. E. *A Dictionary of Symbols.* NY: Philosophical Library, 1978.

Conway, D. J. *The Ancient & Shining Ones.* St. Paul, MN: Llewellyn, 1993.

Conway, D. J. *Animal Magick: The Art of Recognizing & Working With Familiars.* St. Paul, MN: Llewellyn, 1995.

Conway, D. J. *By Oak, Ash & Thorn: Modern Celtic Shamanism.* St. Paul, MN: Llewellyn, 1995.

Conway, D. J. *Dancing With Dragons.* St. Paul, MN: Llewellyn, 1994.

Cooper, J. C. *Symbolic & Mythological Animals.* UK: Aquarian/ Thorsons, 1992.

Cotterell, Arthur. *The Macmillan Illustrated Encyclopedia of Myths & Legends.* NY: Macmillan, 1989.

Cunningham, Scott. *Cunningham's Encyclopedia of Crystal, Gem, and Metal Magic.* St. Paul, MN: Llewellyn Publications, 1987.

Cunningham, Scott. *Cunningham's Encyclopedia of Magical Herbs.* St. Paul, MN: Llewellyn Publications, 1985.

Cunningham, Scott. *Earth Power.* St. Paul, MN: Llewellyn Publications, 1983.

d'Alvielle, Count Goblet. *Migration of Symbols.* UK: Aquarian Press, 1979.

Danielou, Alain. *Hindu Polytheism.* NY: Pantheon Books, 1966.

Davidson, H. R. Ellis. *Gods & Myths of the Viking Age.* NY: Bell Publishing, 1981.

Davidson, H. R. Ellis. *Pagan Scandinavia.* NY: Frederick A. Praeger, 1967.

Dennys, Rodney. *The Heraldic Imagination.* NY: Charles N. Potter, 1975.

Desautels, Paul E. *The Gem Kingdom.* NY: Random House, n.d.

Edwards, Gillian. *Hobgoblin & Sweet Puck.* UK: Bles, 1974.

Erdoes, Richard and Ortiz, Alfonso, ed. *American Indian Myths & Legends.* NY: Pantheon Books, 1984.

Funk, Wildred. *Word Origins & Their Romantic Stories.* NY: Bell Publishing, 1978.

Gimbutas, Marija. *The Language of the Goddess.* San Francisco, CA: Harper-Collins, 1991.

Graves, Robert. *Greek Myths.* UK: Penguin Books, 1981.

Graves, Robert. *The White Goddess.* NY: Farrar, Straus & Giroux, 1981.

Grice, F. *Folk Tales of the North Country.* UK: Nelson, 1944.

Guerber, H. A. *Legends of the Middle Ages.* NY: American Book Co., 1924.

Guerber, H. A. *Legends of the Rhine.* NY: A.S. Barnes & Co., 1895.

Guerber, H. A. *Myths of the Norsemen.* NY: Dover, 1992. Originally published 1909.

Guest, Lady Charlotte, trans. *The Mabinogion.* NY: E.P. Dutton, 1906.

Guirand, Felix, ed. Trans. Richard Aldington and Delano Ames. *New Larousse Encyclopedia of Mythology.* UK: Hamlyn, 1978.

Hall, James. *Dictionary of Subjects & Symbols in Art.* NY: Harper & Row, 1974.

Hall, Manly P. *The Secret Teachings of All Ages.* Los Angeles, CA: Philosophical Research Society, 1977.

Hathaway, Nancy. *The Unicorn.* NY: Avenel, 1980.

Hazlitt, W. Carew. *Faiths & Folklore of the British Isles.* 2 vols. NY: Benjamin Blum, 1965.

Hinnells, John R. *Persian Mythology.* UK: Hamlyn, 1975.

Hooke, S. H. *Babylonian & Assyrian Religion.* UK: Hutchinson, 1953.

Hooke, S. H. *Middle Eastern Mythology.* UK: Penguin Books, 1963.

Huber, Richard. *Treasury of Fantastic & Mythological Creatures.* NY: Dover, 1981.

Huygen, Wil. *Gnomes.* NY: Peacock Press, 1977.

Ions, Veronica. *Indian Mythology.* NY: Paul Hamlyn, 1973.

Jacobson, Helen. *The First Book of Legendary Beings.* NY: Franklin Watts, 1962.

Jobes, Gertrude and James. *Outer Space.* NY: Scarecrow Press, 1964.

Johnson, Buffie. *Lady of the Beasts: Ancient Images of the Goddess & Her Sacred Animals.* San Francisco, CA: Harper & Row, 1981.

Jung, Carl G. Trans. R. F. C. Hull. *The Archetypes and the Collective Unconscious.* NJ: Princeton University Press, 1990.

Jung, Carl G. *Psychology & Alchemy.* NJ: Princeton University Press, 1953.

Keightley, Thomas. *The World Guide to Gnomes, Fairies, Elves & Other Little People.* NY: Avenel Books, 1978. Originally published 1878.

King, Stephen. *Nightmares in the Sky.* NY: Viking Studio Books, 1988.

Kipling, Rudyard. Ed. by John Beecroft. *Kipling: A Selection of His Stories & Poems.* "Puck of Pook's Hill." Garden City, NY: Doubleday & Co., 1956. (Originally published 1892.)

Lawson, John Cuthbert. *Modern Greek Folklore & Ancient Greek Religion.* NY: University Books, 1964.

Legge, Francis. *Forerunners & Rivals of Christianity.* 2 vols. NY: University Books, 1964.

Lethaby, W. R. *Architecture, Mysticism & Myth.* NY: George Braziller, 1975.

Ley, Willy. *The Lungfish, the Dodo & the Unicorn: An Excursion into Romantic Zoology.* NY: Viking, 1948.

Lindsay, Jack. *The Origins of Astrology.* NY: Barnes & Noble, 1971.

Lippman, Deborah & Colin, Paul. *How to Make Amulets, Charms & Talismans.* NY: M. Evans & Co., 1974.

Lum, Peter. *Fabulous Beasts.* NY: Pantheon Books, 1951.

Lurker, Manfred. *Dictionary of Gods & Goddesses, Devils & Demons.* UK: Routledge & Kegan Paul, 1987.

Lurker, Manfred. *The Gods & Symbols of Ancient Egypt.* UK: Thames & Hudson, 1991.

MacKenzie, Donald A. *German Myths & Legends.* NY: Avenel Books, 1985.

Maspero, Gaston. *Popular Stories of Ancient Egypt.* NY: University Books, 1967.

Matthews, John & Caitlin. *The Aquarian Guide to British & Irish Mythology.* UK: Aquarian Press, 1988.

McCoy, Edain. *A Witch's Guide to Faery Folk.* St. Paul, MN: Llewellyn, 1994.

O'Flaherty, Wendy Doniger. *Hindu Myths.* UK: Penguin Books, 1975.

O'Suilleabhain, Sean. *Folktales of Ireland.* UK: Routledge & Kegan Paul, 1966.

Page, Michael & Ingpen, Robert. *Encyclopedia of Things That Never Were.* NY: Viking, 1987.

Pepper, Elizabeth & Wilcock, John. *Magical & Mystical Sites.* NY: Harper & Row, 1977.

Piggott, Juliet. *Japanese Mythology.* UK: Paul Hamlyn, 1975.

Poltarnees, Welleran. *A Book of Unicorns.* La Jolla: Green Tiger Press, 1978.

Potter, Stephen and Sargeant, Laurens. *Pedigree.* NY: Taplinger, 1974.

Robertson, R. MacDonald. *Selected Highland Folktales.* UK: David & Charles, 1977.

Ross, Anne. *The Pagan Celts.* NJ: Barnes & Noble, 1986.

San Souci, Robert S., retold by. *The Firebird.* NY: Dial Books for Young Readers, 1992.

Shepard, Odell. *The Lore of the Unicorn.* NY: Harper & Row, 1979.

Silberer, Herbert. *Hidden Symbolism of Alchemy & the Occult Arts.* NY: Dover, 1971.

Simak, Rudolf. Trans. Angela Hall. *Dictionary of Northern Mythology.* UK: D. S. Brewer, 1993.

Smith, John Holland. *The Death of Classical Paganism.* NY: Scribner, 1976.

South, Malcolm, ed. *Mythical & Fabulous Creatures.* NY: Peter Bedrick Books, 1988.

Spence, Lewis. *British Fairy Origins.* UK: Watts, 1946.

Spence, Lewis. *An Encyclopedia of Occultism.* NY: University Books, 1960.

Spence, Lewis. *The Fairy Traditions in Britain.* UK: Rider, 1948.

Squire, Charles. *Celtic Myth & Legend, Poetry & Romance.* NY: Bell Publishing, 1979.

Stewart, R. J. *Robert Kirk: Walker Between Worlds.* UK: Element Books, 1990.

Stewart, W. Grant. *Popular Superstitions of the Highlanders of Scotland.* UK: Ward Lock, 1970. Originally published 1823.

Sturluson, Snorri. *The Prose Edda.* Berkeley, CA: University of California Press, 1954.

Tatz, Mark and Kent, Jody. *Rebirth.* NY: Anchor Press/Doubleday, 1977.

Thomson, J. Oliver. *History of Ancient Geography.* NY: Biblio & Tannen, 1965.

Toth, Max. *Pyramid Prophecies.* NY: Destiny Books, 1979.

Turville-Petre, E. O. G. *Myth & Religion of the North: The Religion of Ancient Scandinavia.* Westport, CT: Greenwood Press, 1975.

Valiente, Doreen. *Natural Magic.* Custer, WA: Phoenix Publishing, 1985.

Walker, Barbara G. *The Woman's Dictionary of Symbols & Sacred Objects.* San Francisco, CA: Harper & Row, 1988.

Walker, Barbara G. *The Woman's Encyclopedia of Myths & Secrets.* San Francisco, CA: Harper & Row, 1983.

White, T. H., trans. *The Book of Beasts: Being a Translation from a Latin Bestiary of the 12th Century.* NY: Dover, 1984.

Whittick, Arnold. *Symbols: Signs & Their Meaning & Uses in Design.* Newton, MA: Charles T. Branford, 1971.

Williamson, George Hunt. *Secret Places of the Lion.* NY: Warner Destiny Books, 1958.

Wimberly, Lowry Charles. *Folklore in the English & Scottish Ballads.* NY: Dover, 1965.

Yolen, Jane, ed. *Favorite Folktales from Around the World.* NY: Pantheon Books, 1986.

Zimmer, Heinrich. *Myths & Symbols in Indian Art & Civilization.* NJ: Princeton University Press, 1946.

Zipes, Jack, trans. *The Complete Fairy Tales of the Brothers Grimm.* NY: Bantam Books, 1987.

Index

☽ LLEWELLYN ORDERING INFORMATION

Order Online:
Visit our website at www.llewellyn.com, select your books, and order them on our secure server.

Order by Phone:
- Call toll-free within the U.S. at 1-877-NEW-WRLD (1-877-639-9753). Call toll-free within Canada at 1-866-NEW-WRLD (1-866-639-9753)
- We accept VISA, MasterCard, and American Express

Order by Mail:
Send the full price of your order (MN residents add 7% sales tax) in U.S. funds, plus postage & handling to:

Llewellyn Worldwide
P.O. Box 64383, Dept. 0-7387-0294-3
St. Paul, MN 55164-0383, U.S.A.

Postage & Handling:

Standard (U.S., Mexico, & Canada). If your order is:
$49.99 and under, add $3.00
$50.00 and over, FREE STANDARD SHIPPING

AK, HI, PR: $15.00 for one book plus $1.00 for each additional book.

International Orders (airmail only):
$16.00 for one book plus $3.00 for each additional book

Orders are processed within 2 business days.
Please allow for normal shipping time. Postage and handling rates subject to change.

The Celtic Dragon Tarot

D. J. Conway and Lisa Hunt

Are dragons real? Since they do not live on the physical plane, scientists cannot trap and dissect them. Yet magicians and psychics who have explored the astral realms know firsthand that dragons do indeed exist, and that they make very powerful co-magicians. Dragons tap into deeper currents of elemental energies than humans. Because of their ancient wisdom, dragons are valuable contacts to call upon when performing any type of divination, such as the laying out of tarot cards. Tarot decks and other divination tools seem to fascinate them. *The Celtic Dragon Tarot* is the first deck to use the potent energies of dragons for divination, magickal spell working, and meditation.

Ancient mapmakers noted every unknown territory with the phrase "Here be dragons." Both tarot and magick have many uncharted areas. Not only will you discover dragons waiting there, but you will also find them to be extremely helpful when you give them the chance.

1–56718–182–1
Boxed set: 78 full-color cards
with 216 pp., 6 x 9 book   **$29.95**

Shapeshifter Tarot
D. J. CONWAY
AND SIRONA KNIGHT
ILLUSTRATED BY LISA HUNT

Like the ancient Celts, you can now practice the shamanic art of shapeshifting and access the knowledge of the eagle, the oak tree or the ocean: wisdom that is inherently yours and resides within your very being. *The Shapeshifter Tarot* kit is your bridge between humans, animals, and nature. The cards in this deck act as merging tools, allowing you to tap into the many different animal energies, together with the elemental qualities of air, fire, water, and earth.

The accompanying book gives detailed explanations on how to use the cards, along with their full esoteric meanings, and mythological and magical roots. Exercises in shapeshifting, moving through gateways, doubling out, meditation, and guided imagery give you the opportunity to enhance your levels of perception and awareness, allowing you to hone and accentuate your magical understanding and skill.

1–56718–384–0
Boxed kit: 81 full-color cards, instruction book   **$29.95**